PORTALS

PORTALS

GRADE

6

PORTALS

GRADE

6

HOUGHTON MIFFLIN HARCOURT
School Publishers

Opening Up New Worlds

People ask me,

"Where do you come from?"

But they never bother to ask,

"Where are you going?"

You're about to enter *Portals*. This step will open up many new worlds to you. As you study, you'll have a lot of help, but you'll be the one keeping track of the progress you are making. You'll ask and answer questions. You'll decide how you will respond to opportunties. Those decisions are yours, after all. So, where *are* you going?

Recognizing Words

This is a must. Once your know how to identify and pronounce the words you read, you're well on your way. In *Portals*, the pieces of the word puzzle will start to fit together. For example, you'll learn which sound is most likely for a group of letters that has several possible sounds. You'll also learn how to break up very long words in ways that make it easy to pronounce them.

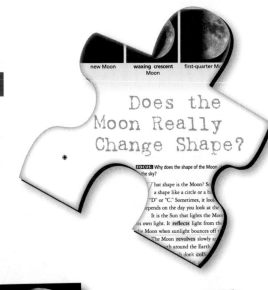

new Moon   waxing crescent   first-quarter Moon
              Moon

Does the Moon Really Change Shape?

FOCUS: Why does the shape of the Moon ... the sky?

... hat shape is the Moon? So... a shape like a circle or a b... "D" or "C." Sometimes, it look... epends on the day you look at the... It is the Sun that lights the Moo... ts own light. It reflects light from th... he Moon when sunlight bounces off ... The Moon revolves slowly a... th around the Earth ... don't colli...

What is the Moon?

The Moon is a natural **satellite**. That means it is a body that is in **orbit**. The Moon **revolves**, or moves around, **planet** Earth. Earth's **gravity** pulls the Moon toward our planet. Therefore, the Moon does not float away into space. If gravity ... we in ... some ti... movem... pull of ... Moon ... Togeth... Earth's ...

How does the Moon look up close?

The Moon look s bright and shiny from down here. It d es not look like that up close. Up close, it looks rather plain and boring. There i no life on the Moon. Plants and ani als cannot survive. It is all a dull, pale rown color. Rocks and dust are every here.

Look closely at the Moon. You can see big, dark **patches** on its surface. People used to think these dark patches were big seas or oceans. Later, scientists found that they are areas that used to be covered with **lava**. That lava is now hard rock.

What are craters?

The surface of the Moon is covered with **craters**. These craters were formed long ago. Big and small **asteroids collided** with the Moon. This made craters. An asteroid is a rock that orbits the sun. Craters on the Moon can be tiny

> Look closely at the Moon. You can see big, dark **patches** on its surface. People used to think these dark patches were big seas or oceans. Later, scientists

The Moon has big rocks.

satellite Any object that revolves around a planet or other larger object.
lava Very hot, melted rock.

asteroid A piece of rock in space.

137

Vocabulary

Learning vocabulary is like so many other things—doing it just once won't make it stick in your mind. When you came to class on the first day of school, you were probably told everyone's name. You didn't remember them all right away, but after a week or so, you did! Learning new words takes a while, too. In *Portals*, you'll have many experiences with each new word. You'll read them, hear them, and work with them in stories, poems, articles, and cartoons. Before you know it, the words—a lot of them—will be yours! You'll own them.

TEKS • 1.A RECOGNIZE WORDS. • 1.B CONFIRM PRONUNCIATIONS AND MEANINGS. • 2.A EXPAND VOCABULARY. • 2.B DETERMINE MEANING THROUGH CONTEXT. • 2.C USE WORD SKILLS TO UNDERSTAND MEANINGS. • 2.D DETERMINE MEANINGS AND PRONUNCIATIONS. • 2.E IDENTIFY WORD RELATIONSHIPS. • 3.A READ SILENTLY. • 3.B ADJUST READING RATE. • 3.C READ ORALLY.

Fluency

You want fluency! It's a reading skill that is important whether you're reading silently or out loud. Fluency is all about reading accurately, getting each word right. It's also about using expression, speaking softly or loudly, sounding excited or sad. Fluency is also rate—how fast or how slowly you read. That will depend on what you're reading. For example, you'll probably read difficult text more slowly, and fun stories more quickly. *Portals* will help you read accurately, with appropriate expression, and at a suitable rate. (You'll also be keeping track of your reading rate as you go through *Portals*.)

Selection 3

from **Home of** e
by Katherine Applegate

FOCUS: What would it be like to move somewhere that is different in every way from your homeland?

Kek comes from an African country torn by war. He has lost most of his family. He is brought to the United States to live with his aunt and his cousin Ganwar. Dave, an American man, helps him get settled. Now all Kek has to do is fit in—somehow!

This story is told as a series of poems. As Kek's words show, things that are ordinary to you can seem very strange to a newcomer.

Snow

When the flying boat
returns to earth at last,
I open my eyes
and **gaze** out the round window.
What is all the white? I whisper.
Where is all the world?

The helping man greets me
and there are many lines and questions
and pieces of paper.

At last I follow him outside.
We call that snow, he says.
Isn't it beautiful?
Do you like the cold?

I want to say
No, this cold is like claws on my skin!
I look around me.
Dead grass pokes through
the unkind blanket of white.

176 ▶ DAY 8

I like the way the surface of the water reflects the patches of light.

ELPS • 2.C LEARN NEW EXPRESSIONS AND VOCABULARY THROUGH LISTENING. • 2.D MONITOR UNDERSTANDING OF SPOKEN LANGUAGE. • 2.G UNDERSTAND SPOKEN LANGUAGE. • 2.H UNDERSTAND IMPLICIT IDEAS IN SPOKEN LANGUAGE. • 2.I DEMONSTRATE LISTENING COMPREHENSION. • 3.D INTERNALIZE VOCABULARY THROUGH SPEAKING. • 3.E SHARE INFORMATION IN COOPERATIVE LEARNING INTERACTIONS. • 4.C DEVELOP BASIC SIGHT VOCABULARY.

Purposes for Reading

There are countless things to read and many reasons to read them. Suppose you're looking for information. You might read a nonfiction book or a newspaper. If you're reading for entertainment, you might pick a novel or short story. If you want to solve a problem, you might first try using a search engine on the Internet. Knowing what you want to get from your reading will help you choose what to read and how to read it.

TEKS • 6.A READ FOR VARIOUS PURPOSES. • 6.B READ SOURCES. • 6.C USE VISUAL REPRESENTATIONS. • 4.A USE PRIOR KNOWLEDGE AND EXPERIENCE. • 4.B DETERMINE PURPOSE FOR READING. • 4.C SELF-MONITOR READING AND ADJUST. • 4.D SUMMARIZE TEXTS. • 4.E MAKE INFERENCES. • 4.F ANALYZE AND USE TEXT STRUCTURES. • 4.G MAKE CONNECTIONS ACROSS TEXTS. • 4.H CONSTRUCT VISUAL IMAGES. • 4.I DETERMINE IMPORTANT IDEAS. • 4.J MANAGE TEXT. • 4.K USE QUESTIONING TO ENHANCE COMPREHENSION.

Comprehension

There are a lot of reading skills to learn, but don't be put off. You probably know most of these skills already, even if you don't know their names.

- You turn the door handle, open the door, and walk outside. The order in which things happen is called *sequence*. First you turn the door handle, then you open the door. . . well, you get the idea.

- It starts to rain. The street gets wet. That's called *cause and effect*. The rain is the cause. The wet street is the effect.

- While you wait for the school bus, you tell your friend the story of the movie you saw yesterday. Maybe you didn't know that you just gave a *summary*, but you did.

You'll apply your comprehension skills throughout *Portals*. You'll find out that authors don't always present things the way you might find them in real life. Events may not be written in order, or an effect may be described before you know its cause. *Portals* will help you put all the pieces of the comprehension puzzle together. Comprehension means understanding, and that's the big idea when you read!

ELPS • 3.G EXPRESS OPINIONS, IDEAS, AND FEELINGS. • 3.H NARRATE, DESCRIBE, AND EXPLAIN. • 4.G DEMONSTRATE COMPREHENSION OF TEXT. • 4.I. EMPLOY BASIC READING SKILLS. • 4.J EMPLOY INFERENTIAL SKILLS. • 4.K EMPLOY ANALYTICAL SKILLS.

RELATIVE SIZE OF THE SUN AND PLANETS

JUPITER   SATURN   URANUS   NEPTUNE

Finding Information

It's the twenty-first century, and finding information is easier than ever. Even so, you need to ask the right questions to get the right answers. *Portals* will help you come up with the right questions and find the right sources for the information you want. You'll use diagrams and charts to understand complicated ideas easily. You'll even be asked to watch television programs and videos as parts of your research! You'll also have plenty of practice presenting the information you find to other people.

Evaluating Credibility

As you research various topics, you'll want to know whether you can trust your sources. *Portals* will help you figure out how trustworthy a source is, especially on the Internet. You'll also learn how writers can try to persuade you. (Sometimes they do it for a good cause, but not always!)

You'll also discover when an argument that sounds reasonable shouldn't convince you. Here's an example:

My cat catches mice.
Squeaky is a mouse.
So, my cat will catch Squeaky.

It sounds right, but it isn't.
We'll tell you why it isn't right.

TEKS • 5.A GENERATE QUESTIONS. • 5.B LOCATE INFORMATION. • 5.C ORGANIZE AND RECORD NEW INFORMATION. • 5.D COMMUNICATE INFORMATION GAINED FROM READING. • 5.E RAISE ADDITIONAL QUESTIONS. • 5.F USE TEXT ORGANIZERS. • 8.A EVALUATE CREDIBILITY AND RELEVANCE. • 8.B EVALUATE WRITER'S MOTIVATION. • 8.C ANALYZE TEXT FOR PERSUASIVE EFFECT. • 8.D RECOGNIZE MODES OF REASONING. • 8.F RECOGNIZE LOGICAL AND ILLOGICAL ARGUMENTS. • 7.A RESPOND ACTIVELY TO TEXTS.

Responding to Text

After you've read something, then what?
Often you'll be asked whether or not you
liked what you read, but you'll also be
asked why. *Portals* will help you discuss
and write about what you've read. You'll
use your own knowledge and experience
to support your responses, and you'll also
quote and give details from texts.

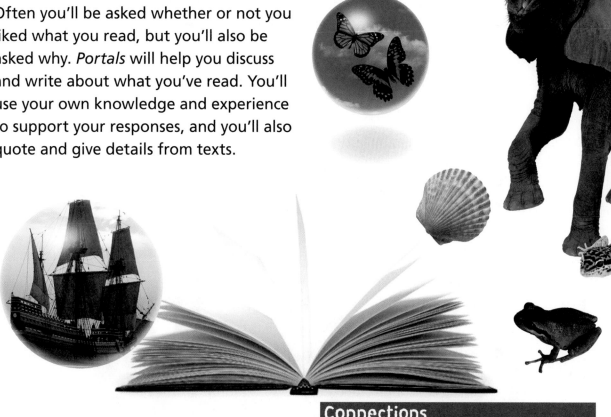

Connections

The reading selections in *Portals* cover
a lot of different topics and styles. In
many of them, you'll find events that
relate to your own experiences or
those of your friends. You'll see how
many different cultures have the same
kinds of stories. As you learn about
other cultures, you'll see what they
have in common with your own
culture. You'll understand the world
better, and you'll understand your
place in it better, too.

• 7.B RESPOND TO TEXT. • 7.C SUPPORT RESPONSES. •
9.A COMPARE TEXT EVENTS WITH EXPERIENCES. •
9.B RECOGNIZE THEMES AND CONNECTIONS THAT CROSS
CULTURES.

Selection **1**

THE CROW AND
THE WATER JUG

a fable adapted by Eve Rice

FOCUS: How can starting small help y...

Crow has a **task** *that may be too big! So she will s...
will get done.*

One day thirsty Crow came upon a wate...
"Now I will have a drink," she th...
She put her beak in the jug, but...
could not get a drink.
So she reached farther in. She flapp...
her neck.
But still she could not get a single drop to drink.
"I know," she thought. "I'll turn the jug over on its side." And
then she pushed with all her might.
But no matter how she tried, the jug still stood upright.

from the Plains I... an Museum
C... an r settled hers
...any years a...
...nera...

The lessons and the selections in *Portals* go together in a way that makes sense. The pieces have all been put together.

Portals will help you get to where you're going.

TABLE OF CONTENTS

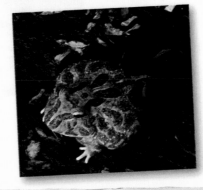

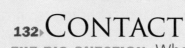

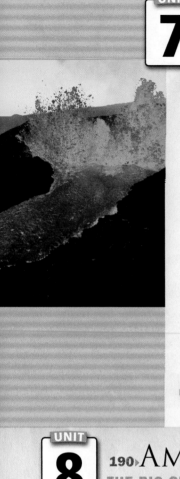

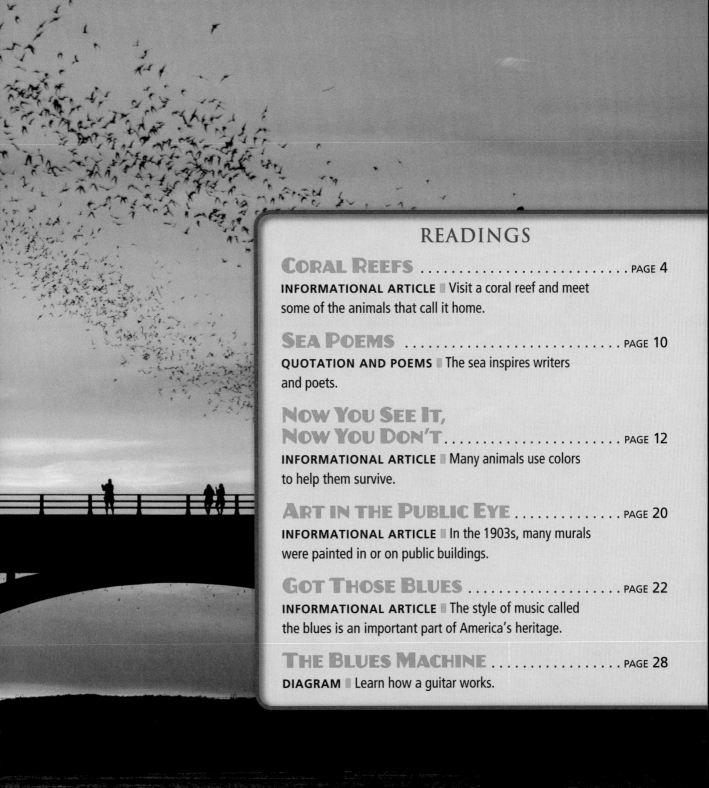

READINGS

Coral Reefs

This "big leaf" is a sea fan.

FOCUS: What can you find in a coral reef?

LOOK IT UP

For more information on coral reefs: tropical waters, barrier reef, parrotfish, angelfish, clown fish, coral reef food chain, coral reef conservation, coral reef habitat

A reef is a big coral ridge. It sits in shallow water, so it is lit up by the sun.

Coral can be as hard as a rock. It can grow in fun shapes. A sea fan is a big coral mass. It is tall but narrow. It can look like a fan or a wide, slim leaf.

Coral may look like a plant. But it isn't one. It is made up of animals, each as big as a bug!

A lot of sea animals can live in a reef. Fish, rays, and eels all fill it with color.

5

Parrotfish

A parrotfish has a beak like a parrot. It will eat algae off a reef. It will use its beak to cut bits of coral off as well. So you may think a parrotfish can harm a reef. But, in fact, it helps. Algae can sometimes cover up a reef and kill it. A parrotfish can help a reef by keeping algae at bay.

A parrotfish has a sharp beak.

A ray can have a long tail.

Rays

A ray can live in a reef as well. A ray is a big flat fish. It has no bones. It has big fins. A ray can be huge. It can be more than 20 feet wide! Fish that live in the reef help keep a ray healthy. Angelfish will swim inside the ray's gills and eat the dead skin cells and tiny animals. This helps the ray and gives the angelfish a good meal.

An eel waits for a meal.

Eels

Eels can live in rock beds by a reef. An eel will feed on sea animals in the reef. It will hide in rocks waiting patiently. When its prey is close by, it will leap up and kill it. An eel does not see well. But it has a keen nose. So it can smell if a meal is swimming by.

REREAD

Description

What does this paragraph describe?

8

Visit a Reef

On a clear day, you can go visit a reef. You can go by boat. You can swim in the reef. But if you see a "pretty rock," you must not pick it up. It may be a live animal! If you take an animal out of its home, it may die. So be careful!

BAY REEF

FOLLOW MY LEAD!

Set sail with me!
I'll take you to see Bay Reef.

It is not far away.
If we hop on a boat, we'll be there in a snap.

We'll soak in the hot sun.
We'll dip in and see Bay Reef!
We'll see fish, rays, and eels!
We'll see corals in red, tan, and teal!
It'll put a smile on your face!

Call me at 555-6655. I'll set you up.

Pam Beal
Bay Reef, Inc.

STOP AND THINK

1. What fills a coral reef with color?

2. If you could visit Bay Reef, what would you like to see?

From the Sea

Sea Poems

FOCUS: What about the sea, or other bodies of water, draws people to them?

> "Yes, I love it.
> The sea is everything."
>
> — Jules Verne,
>
> *20,000 Leagues Under the Sea*

Sea Shell

Sea Shell, Sea Shell,
Sing me a song, O please!
A song of ships, and sailor men,
And parrots, and tropical trees,

Of islands lost in the Spanish Main
Which no man ever may find again,
Of fishes and corals under the waves,
And sea horses stabled in great green caves.

Sea Shell, Sea Shell,
Sing of the things you know so well.

Amy Lowell

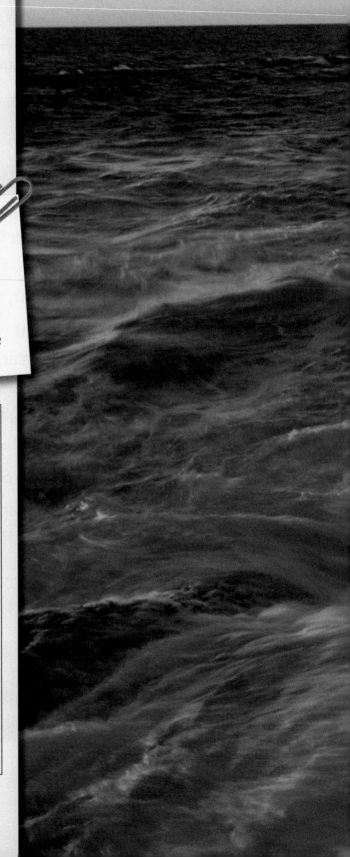

Until I Saw the Sea

Until I saw the sea
I did not know
that wind
could wrinkle water so.

I never knew
that sun
could splinter a whole sea of blue.

Nor
did I know before,
a sea breathes in and out
upon a shore.

Lilian Moore

STOP AND THINK

1. How can a shell appear to sing, as in the poem by Amy Lowell?

2. Lilian Moore compares crashing waves to the act of breathing. What else about a beach or shoreline seems alive?

Now You See It, Now You Don't!

LOOK IT UP

For more on animal camouflage: Leaf-tailed gecko camouflage, katydids camouflage, dead leaf butterfly, Indonesian mimic octopus, leafy sea dragon

FOCUS: How does color help animals survive?

If something blends in with its surroundings, it is hard to spot. In the wild, a lot of animals use this trick to hide. If an animal is the same color as its home, others cannot find it. This means it can sneak up on its prey. Or it can hide and make sure nothing eats *it*. This colorful game of hide-and-seek can keep an animal alive!

A shrimp on a sea slug

The Imperial Shrimp

An Imperial Shrimp can be a bold red color. It often joins up with a sea slug that is also red. The sea slug has big gills that move and fold. As the sea slug swims, the shrimp hides in these folds. It blends in with its bright red surroundings, so animals that eat shrimp will not find it. Because it matches its host's color so well, this shrimp will not be harmed.

The Arctic Fox

An Arctic fox is at home in snow and ice. It has a deep, thick coat that helps it keep warm. In fall and winter, this coat is white. So when a fox curls up, it looks just like a pile of snow.

This means that a fox will stay safe if it takes a nap on a snowdrift. Also, when it goes hunting, it can sneak up on its prey. The fox blends in well with the cold, snowy landscape. So animals it hunts will not see it coming.

REREAD

Problem/Solution

What problem does the fox have?

In springtime, the weather is not so cold. Days become mild, and the snow melts. A white fox cannot hide well during this time. But an Arctic fox is not always white. In mild weather, this fox's pelt will turn gray. Its new coat blends in with the dirt and brush. By matching its surroundings, this fox can hide all year long.

A fox curled up in the snow

A crab spider on a yellow flower

The Crab Spider

A crab spider can also change color to match its surroundings. When it sits on a yellow flower, its body changes to a yellow hue. But when it sits on a white flower, it becomes white!

The crab spider uses this trick when it hunts. This spider matches its surroundings so well that bugs do not see it. So a bug will come quite close.

The spider does not mind waiting. It can sit still for days without making a noise. It holds its front legs up, ready to grab a passing bug. It waits and waits till a bug is close by.

Then it strikes! It darts out and catches a bug with its front legs. It can catch a fly. It can catch a butterfly. It can even kill and eat a bee.

The Three-Toed Sloth

A sloth spends a lot of time hanging upside down in a tree. It has big hooks on its feet that it uses to hold onto branches and vines. A sloth chews on leaves, buds, and twigs that it finds in its tree.

The sloth got its name because it moves so slowly. It can take a whole day to crawl from one tree to another. This means that if a predator comes by, a sloth is in trouble. If a wildcat spots it, the sloth cannot run away. So how can a sloth stay safe?

Green algae and mold grow in a sloth's pelt. Each hair has a groove that holds algae. This gives a sloth a moss-green tint, just like the tree it lives in. Wildcats that prowl the forest floor and hawks that soar through the air cannot see it. It is the sloth's coloring that keeps it safe!

A sloth in a tree

■■■ STOP AND THINK

1. Which animals use color to hide?

2. Do people also use color to hide? Explain.

Comprehension

✔ **TARGET SKILL** **Main Idea and Details** Every passage or selection contains a topic that can usually be stated in just a few words. A topic is what a passage or selection is about. Passages and selections also contain a main idea. A main idea is the most important idea about the topic. Usually the main idea can be stated in a sentence. Sometimes it is stated in a sentence that comes near the beginning or the end of a passage or a selection. Other times, readers must figure out the main idea from details provided in the selection. Details are small bits of information found in a passage or a selection. Details that support or tell more about the main idea are called supporting details.

The following paragraph, taken from the selection "Art in the Public Eye" is about the topic of WPA murals. It contains both a main idea and details that support that main idea.

This sentence tells the main idea of the paragraph.

The WPA did not tell artists what to paint, but they did encourage certain themes. They wanted artists to paint about positive, "American" ideals. Many murals show American landscapes and customs. They show ordinary people succeeding through hard work.

The other sentences tell details that support the main idea. They tell specifically what content the WPA wanted.

18

Topic:
content of the WPA murals

Main Idea:
The WPA encouraged American themes in the murals.

- positive, "American" ideals
- American landscapes and customs
- ordinary people succeeding through hard work

TARGET STRATEGY **Summarize** A summary sums up a story. When you summarize, you tell in your own words what a selection is about. Summarizing can help you remember the important ideas in a selection.

Art in the Public Eye

FOCUS: Why should art be available to everyone?

In the early 1930s, America was suffering. People were sad, hungry, and desperate for work. It was the middle of the Great Depression. Something had to change.

Politicians wondered how to make things right. One of the best efforts was President Franklin D. Roosevelt's New Deal. His programs created jobs and fueled new hope.

This was a grueling time. It was hard for anyone to find work. Artists were especially unlikely to find jobs. With this in mind, the Works Progress Administration and other groups funded public art projects. They gave jobs to thousands of artists. They also created works of art that everyone could enjoy.

The murals served many purposes. They made fine art available to everyone at no cost. The colorful murals entertained and informed. They also provided distraction from bleak, troubled days.

The WPA did not tell artists what to paint, but they did encourage certain themes. They wanted artists to paint about positive, "American" ideals. Many murals show American landscapes

■ **South Texas Panorama, 1939, by Warren Hunter (Alice, Texas, Post Office)**

and customs. They show ordinary people succeeding through hard work.

Sometimes, artists had to compete for jobs. Then the agency director would pick the best one. One such winner was Warren Hunter. In 1939, he painted a vast mural in the Alice, Texas, Post Office. It shows men and women working hard to better their lives. The mural stayed in place until 1969. At that point, Hunter himself removed it—along with half the wall! He had it placed in the Smithsonian museum. You can still visit it there today.

Another great muralist of the time was Maxine Albro. She worked on many public projects, including one in San Francisco's Coit Tower. The tower houses murals by quite a few artists, all funded by the WPA. Albro's mural shows farmers making their living off American soil. Albro painted bright subjects in fiery colors. Her mural still exists in its California location today.

By 1943, America had changed. World War II had started. The economy had picked up. The WPA had come to an end. But this program, and others like it, left behind a huge body of work. In less than 10 years, the government had funded about 4,000 murals. We can still enjoy most of them to this day.

■ **California Agriculture, 1934, by Maxine Albro (Coit Tower, San Fransico)**

STOP AND THINK

1. How did the New Deal murals affect Americans?

2. If you were painting a mural in your school, what would you paint?

GOT THOSE BLUES

FOCUS: Why do people sing the blues?

When a friend says that he has "the blues," it means that he is unhappy. But this phrase can also refer to a style of music. A blues song is often about grief. It may be about bad luck or a lost love. It may be about a hard job or a mean boss. But it can have jokes in it, too. So if you are blue, singing a blues song may make you feel a bit better!

The blues got its name back in the early 1900s. But we can trace the roots of the blues back to the days of slavery in the Deep South. Enslaved men and women sang and prayed while loading cotton bales and tending crops in the field. They sang about real life and the pain of slavery. These were the first blues songs.

WHAT MAKES A BLUES SONG?

The shape of a blues song is quite simple. It has three lines that make up its frame. We can call the first line *A*. Line *A* is sung twice. Then we add a Line *B*. So a blues song has an *AAB* shape, like this song by Langston Hughes:

A→ Oh, the sun is so hot and the day is so doggone long ...

A→ Yes, the sun is so hot and the day is so doggone long ...

B→ And that is the reason I'm singing this doggone song.

This song has the same shape:

A→ I can still see that train fly on down that track.

A→ Yep, I can still see that train fly on down that track.

B→ My heart is crying. My sweet gal's not coming back!

REREAD

Sequence

What happens after the first line?

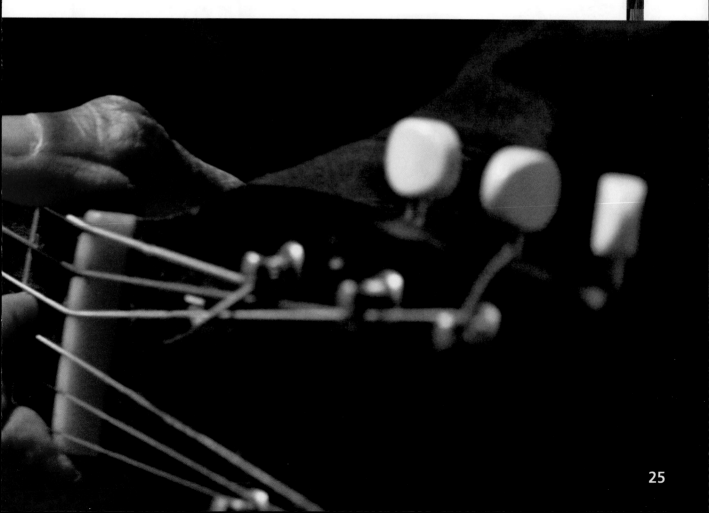

A blues singer sings from the heart. A tune
can be made up on the spot. As long as a song keeps
its basic shape, you can sing it any way you like. It
can be slow and soft. It can be loud and fast. Any
way you sing it, it is still a blues song.

The blues is a big part of music we hear today.
We can hear the influence of the blues in ragtime,
swing, bebop, rock, hip-hop, R&B, and pop.

B. B. KING CAN PLAY!

B. B. King is the "king of the blues." He writes songs, sings, and plays guitar. He likes his guitars so much that he names them! He names each one "Lucille."

B. B. has his own unique playing style. He bends and slides the strings so that his notes seem to sing. As B. B. once said, "When I sing, I play in my mind; the minute I stop singing...I start to sing by playing Lucille." He meant that his guitar notes are like a second voice to him.

As a child, B. B. played on street corners for dimes. He started recording albums in the 1940s.

STOP AND THINK

1. What is the form of a blues song?

2. What is a good topic for a blues song?

The Blues Machine

FOCUS: How does a guitar work?

A guitar is part of most blues, country, rock, and pop songs you hear. A guitar can help describe a lover's heartbreak. It can put you in the mood to dance. It can make the toil of a boring job go more quickly. A guitar can tell a musical story.

Every song you listen to is made up of different notes. You can make these notes with a guitar. If you place your fingers on a guitar's neck and then strum, you will hear notes. The higher up the neck you go—the closer to the bridge—the higher the note. The lower down the neck you go, the lower the note.

What makes the high or low sound you hear? If you pick a guitar string, it vibrates, or "shivers." The vibration goes down the neck to the bridge. The bridge spreads the vibration over the soundboard, making the sound that you hear coming out of the sound hole.

Do you know how to play, or want to learn? You're on your way!

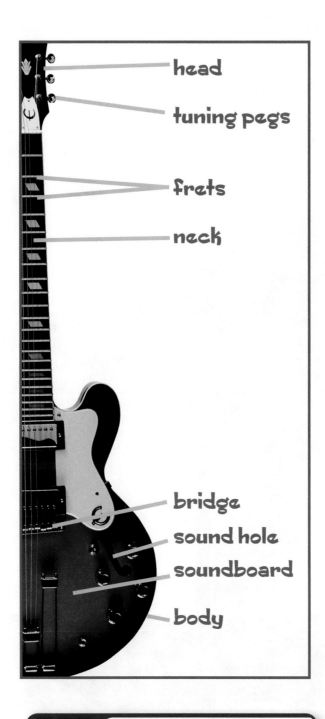

head

tuning pegs

frets

neck

bridge

sound hole

soundboard

body

STOP AND THINK

1. On which part of the guitar do you find the frets?

2. Which musical instrument would you like to learn more about?

UNIT 2

STARTING SMALL

THE BIG QUESTION:
HOW CAN TAKING SMALL STEPS HELP YOU REACH A BIG GOAL?

READINGS

What can we use to make small things look bigger?

To make small things look bigger we can use...

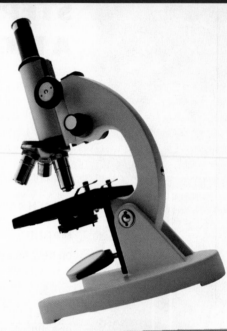

- ☐ a telescope.
- ☐ a magnifying glass.
- ☐ a microscope.
- ☐ a pair of eyeglasses.

What small signs tell you the season is changing?

Small signs that show the season is changing are...

- ☐ a change in temperature.
- ☐ a change in daylight hours.
- ☐ the arrival or departure of birds.
- ☐ a change in trees and other plants.

How can you include someone you don't trust in a project?

You can include someone you don't trust by...

☐ letting him or her plan the project.

☐ giving him or her a lot of responsibility.

☐ giving him or her a small task to do.

☐ putting him or her in charge.

What can we do with shoes and clothing that are too small?

Shoes and clothing that are too small can be...

☐ thrown away.

☐ worn anyway.

☐ given to people who can fit into them.

☐ put in the back of a closet.

33

Literature Words

grain

magnify

makeshift

pebble

shingle

stylish

task

transfix

universe

wit

grain

A **grain** is a small hard particle, such as a a grain of sand or crystal.

" If you look closely at a grain of salt, you can see that it is a crystal. "

magnify

Magnify means increase the size of something.

" The microscope will magnify the cells so that we can see them. "

stylish

Stylish means having elegance, taste, or refinement in dress or manners.

" She always wears stylish clothes to work. "

task

A **task** is a piece of work that is assigned to or expected of a person.

" His task was to walk the dog each morning. "

makeshift

Makeshift refers to something done or made using whatever is available.

66 When they became lost in the woods, the hikers put together a makeshift shelter. 99

pebble

A **pebble** is a small round stone, especially one worn smooth by the action of water.

66 While walking along the beach, Jon found a beautiful green pebble. 99

shingle

A **shingle** is a thin piece of material that is laid in overlapping rows to cover roofs or walls of buildings.

66 He replaced a shingle on the roof to stop the leaking. 99

transfix

Transfix means to make or hold motionless with amazement, awe, or terror.

66 Her act on the trapeze will transfix the audience. 99

universe

The **universe** is all matter and energy, including Earth, galaxies, and the contents of space.

66 The Hubble telescope allows scientists to study the universe. 99

wit

Wit refers to cleverness or intelligence.

66 The woman coaxed the cat down from the tree by wit, not strength. 99

Keys to the Universe

by Francisco X. Alarcón

my Grandpa
Pancho
taught us

my brothers
my sisters
and me

our first
letters
in Spanish

his living
room was
our classroom

"and these are
the true keys
to the **universe**"

he'd tell us
pointing to
the letters

of the alphabet
on the **makeshift**
blackboard

36

March

by Elizabeth Coatsworth

A blue day,
a blue jay
and a good beginning.

One crow,
melting snow—
spring's winning!

magnifying glass

by Valerie Worth

Small **grains**
In a stone
Grow edges
That twinkle;

The smooth
Moth's wing
Sprouts feathers
Like **shingles**;

My thumb
Is wrapped
In rich
Satin wrinkles.

THE CROW AND THE WATER JUG

a fable adapted by Eve Rice

FOCUS: How can starting small help you reach a goal?

Crow has a **task** *that may be too big! So she will start small. Then the job will get done.*

One day thirsty Crow came upon a water jug.

"Now I will have a drink," she thought.

She put her beak in the jug, but the water was so low, Crow could not get a drink.

So she reached farther in. She flapped her wings and stretched her neck.

But still she could not get a single drop to drink.

"I know," she thought. "I'll turn the jug over on its side." And then she pushed with all her might.

But no matter how she tried, the jug still stood upright.

"I may as well give up," she thought. And Crow might have flown away—but she stopped and thought again.

A moment later, Crow bent down and picked up a **pebble**. She dropped it in the jug and then she bent and picked another... One by one, on and on, she dropped the pebbles in the jug.

And with each stone that she dropped in, the water rose a little bit until, at last, it reached the top.

"Caw, caw!" Crow called and had her drink. "Caw, caw!" Crow called and flapped her wings. For she had learned that many things are better done bit by bit. And things that can't be done by strength may often be done by wit .

STOP AND THINK

1. Why was thinking small the best way to solve Crow's problem?

2. When do you find it useful to break a problem down into small steps?

39

Comprehension

✔ **TARGET SKILL** **Story Structure** Some stories are written to entertain readers. Others are written to teach a lesson about life. Most stories have *characters*, a *setting*, and a *plot*. The plot centers around a problem that the main character tries to solve. The plot begins with the **rising action**, which tells about the problem and the character's attempts to solve it. These events lead up to a **climax**, which is the point at which the main character solves the problem. What happens after the climax is called the **falling action**, which leads towards the **resolution**, or ending.

The following excerpts are taken from the fable "The Crow and the Water Jug."

She put her beak in the jug, but the water was so low, Crow could not get a drink.

So she reached farther in. She flapped her wings and stretched her neck.

> This is the **rising action** of the story. It tells about the main character Crow and her problem. The rising action also shows Crow's attempts to reach the water.

"I know," she thought. "I'll turn the jug over on its side." And then she pushed with all her might.

But no matter how hard she tried, the jug still stood upright.

A moment later, Crow bent down and picked up a pebble. She dropped it in the jug and then she bent and picked another... One by one, on and on, she dropped the pebbles in the jug.

And with each stone that she dropped in, the water rose a little bit until, at last, it reached the top.

> Crow finally solves her problem. Now she will be able to get a drink of water. This is the **climax** of the story's plot.

The plot line shows the events that make up the rising action, climax, and falling action of "The Crow and the Water Jug."

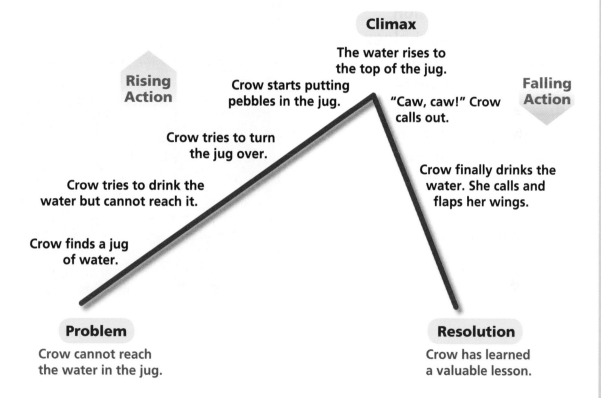

Climax

The water rises to the top of the jug.

Rising Action

Crow starts putting pebbles in the jug.

"Caw, caw!" Crow calls out.

Falling Action

Crow tries to turn the jug over.

Crow finally drinks the water. She calls and flaps her wings.

Crow tries to drink the water but cannot reach it.

Crow finds a jug of water.

Problem

Crow cannot reach the water in the jug.

Resolution

Crow has learned a valuable lesson.

✔ TARGET STRATEGY **Summarize** A summary of a story focuses on the main character, the setting, and the important events of the plot. As you read, ask yourself the following questions:

• Who is the main character?

• Where and when does the story take place?

• What important events happen in the story?

These ideas and details will help you summarize the story.

Your Turn

Use Your Words:

brochure	mission
company	psychology
demonstrate	regret
direction	reverse
dud	screech
embroider	solemn
gesture	whine
impress	

- Read the words on the list.
- Read the dialogue. Find the words.

Arts

Don't look so <u>solemn</u>. Finish what you start. That's good <u>psychology</u>.

I'm on a <u>mission</u> to finish this ship. But I <u>regret</u> that I started it.

MORE ACTIVITIES

1. Take a Survey

Graphic Organizer

Ask ten classmates what their favorite arts-and-crafts activity is. Tally their answers in a chart. Share your findings with the class.

Favorite Arts and Crafts Activity

Activity	Number of people

2. Write Directions

Writing

Think of a simple task you do well. Write directions for the task. Share the directions with your partner. Talk about ways you can make the directions clearer.

3. Dialogue
Listening and Speaking

Draw a picture of a design you could embroider. Share your design with your partner.

4. Play "Guess It"
Listening and Speaking

One player thinks of a craft. The other player asks up to five yes-or-no questions to try to figure out what it is.

5. You Are the Author
Writing

Did you ever get a toy or gift that was a dud? Write a short poem telling about it.

6. Make a List
Vocabulary

Make a list of all the supplies you might find in an arts-and-crafts classroom. Share your list with your class.

THESE SHOES OF MINE

A PLAY BY GARY SOTO

FOCUS: Have you ever found that a small object feels hugely important to you?

All Manuel wants is a pair of new shoes. Is that too much to ask? But while his sister has saved up her money for shopping, he's spent his money on things like ice cream for his friends. Manuel's wishes and hopes are small at first. But as time goes on, he starts to see the big picture.

Main Characters:
Manuel
Mother
Angel, a bully
Ceci, Manuel's girlfriend
Tío José, Manuel's uncle

Manuel (*to audience*): Mom's always helping relatives from Mexico. (*Mocking*) "Please, stay with us. Don't worry. We have room for you." And me? I get stuck with old shoes or ... (*looking at table piled with sewing, among it a patched-up pair of old pants*) or jeans like these.

(*Lights fade, then come up on Manuel and his mother. Manuel holds up a pair of brand-new loafers.*)

Mother: Take care of them. They're for your birthday, except early.

Manuel: Thanks, Mom! They're really nice.

(He hugs his mother, kicks off his old shoes, and starts to put on the new loafers.)

Mother: They're called loafers. *Mira*, you can put pennies in them.

Manuel: Where?

Mother: Here. In these slots. *(Bends to put in pennies.)* That's why they're called penny loafers.

(Manuel clicks the heels of his penny loafers; Mother leaves stage.)

Manuel: But why should I put pennies in? I'd rather have dimes!

*(Manuel bends to insert two shiny dimes in the slots. He walks around the stage, admiring his shoes. **Transfixed** by the shoes, he doesn't notice Angel, the school bully, who has come onstage.)*

Angel: There's something different about you… *(Circles Manuel.)* How come you're wearing those kind of shoes? You look like a nerd, homes.

Manuel: They're penny loafers. **Stylish** , huh?

Angel *(pointing)*: What's that?

Manuel: What's what?

Angel: That shine! Looks like dimes. Give 'em up!

Manuel *(whining)*: Angel.

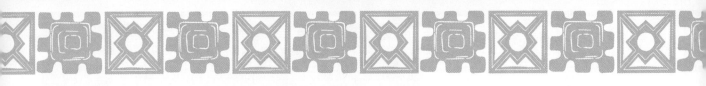

Manuel squeezes the dimes from his shoes. He hands the dimes over to Angel, who leaves, flipping the coins. Manuel walks dejectedly back to his house. He takes the shoes off and throws them into a box.

Manuel (*to audience*): Months pass. My mom keeps taking in relatives from Mexico, and I keep on wearing my old shoes.

(Relatives march in a line across the stage; then his mother appears holding a letter. She sniffs the letter.)

Manuel (*to audience*): And you know what else happens? I grow two inches. I get big. I can feel my shoulders rise like mountains . . . well, more like hills. But still, they get bigger. . . . Then, I get an invitation.

Mother: Manuel, here's a letter ... from a girl.

Manuel: A girl wrote to me?

Mother (*holding it under the light*): Yeah, it says—

Manuel: Mom! It's personal!

(Manuel takes the letter from his mother, who leaves stage.)

Manuel: Wow! An invitation to Ceci's birthday party. "Games and dancing" and "Dress to **impress**."

(Manuel runs offstage. Mother and Tío José, a Mexican immigrant, enter.)

Mother: Let me show you your room. You'll share it with Manuel.

Tío José (*looking about*): Nice place, *¡Y que grande!*

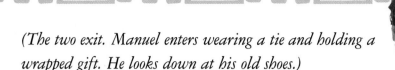

(The two exit. Manuel enters wearing a tie and holding a wrapped gift. He looks down at his old shoes.)

Manuel: I can't wear these shoes.

(He turns to the box holding his loafers. He takes out the loafers, fits in two dimes, and then struggles to put them on.)

Manuel: Hmmm, kind of tight. Guess my feet were growing with the rest of me.

(Manuel walks around stage, taking hurtful steps.)

Manuel: But I got to go to the party! It's going to be a good one.

(Manuel walks painfully, crawls, swims, then gets back to his feet.)

Manuel: Maybe if I walk backward, my toes won't feel so jammed.

(Manuel begins to walk backward, sighing with relief.)

Manuel: Wow, the world looks different. The birds look different, and the cars, and those kids over there on their bikes.

(As Manuel absorbs the world in his backward walk, Ceci and partygoers come onstage. Manuel bumps into Ceci.)

Manuel: Sorry, Ceci.

Ceci: That's okay. How come you're walking backward?

Manuel: Oh, you know, to see how the world looks from the other **direction**. *(Pause)* Also, I'm inventing a dance.

Ceci: You're what?

Manuel: A new dance. It's called … the Backward Caterpillar.

*(Manuel **demonstrates** by cha-cha-ing backward. Ceci and partygoers fall in line and cha-cha backward, too.)*

Ceci: Look at Manuel slide in his new shoes!

(Partygoers ad-lib "Cool shoes," "Look at the dude slide," "Manuel's the best!" Partygoers cha-cha off the stage. Lights dim, then come up on Manuel and Tío José in their beds, ready to go to sleep, their hands folded behind their heads.)

Manuel: Doesn't that crack on the ceiling look like lightning?

Tío José: *Sí*, it does. And that one over there looks like a pair of scissors, *¿qué no? (Pause)* You have a good life, *muchacho*. A nice house and plenty to eat. Your mama's a good cook.

Manuel: I am lucky. And I had good luck at Ceci's party.

Tío José *(getting up)*: Wish me luck tomorrow. I'm going to Modesto. I think I got a job in a restaurant there.

Manuel: How will you get there?

(Tío José sits up.)

Tío José *(hooking thumb into a "hitchhiking" manner)*: *Un poquito de éste* and lots of walking. *Pero mira, mis huaraches son* **rasquachis**. *(Laughing)* I hope they can make it to Modesto.

Mother *(offstage)*: José! *Teléfono!*

(When Tío José leaves, Manuel examines his uncle's worn sandals. Manuel scribbles a note as lights dim. Lights come up on Tío José and Manuel asleep; Tío José rises, sleepily rubbing his face. A rooster crows offstage.)

....

rasquachis beaten up or worn out

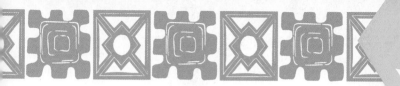

Tío José: It's morning already. *(Eyes Manuel's shiny shoes at foot of bed.)* What's this?

(Tío José reads note and shakes his nephew awake.)

Tío José: These shoes? For me? They're too nice for a worker like me.

Manuel: You have a long way to go, Tío, and you need good shoes.

*(Tío José is touched by this **gesture**. He puts on shoes and walks a few steps as he tries them out.)*

Tío José: They're perfect. *Adiós*, Manuel. These shoes will take me a long ways, and by the time they are worn out, you'll be as tall as your parents. They'll be looking up to you.

(Tío José walks offstage and Manuel lowers his head back onto the pillow.)

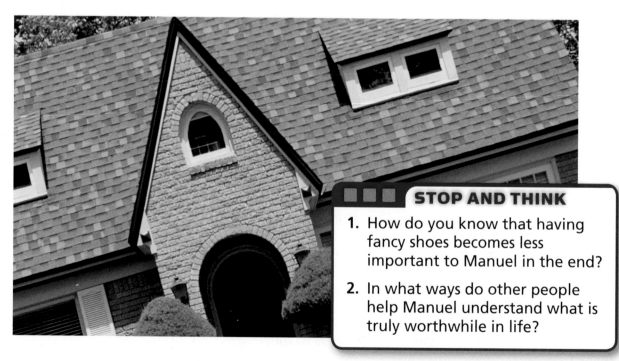

STOP AND THINK

1. How do you know that having fancy shoes becomes less important to Manuel in the end?

2. In what ways do other people help Manuel understand what is truly worthwhile in life?

the project starts small

From **Project Mulberry** *by Linda Sue Park*

Close-up of silkworm moths and their eggs on mulberry leaves

FOCUS: Why is it sometimes worth waiting to see how something small turns out?

Julia and Patrick have a plan for winning a blue ribbon at the state fair—they will raise silkworms! Julia's mother used to do this back in Korea. They'll use the cocoons to make silk thread, which Julia will use to **embroider** *a design.*

Julia and Patrick ordered silkworm eggs through the mail and even found a mulberry tree growing in town. (Silkworms eat only fresh mulberry leaves.) They set up the eggs in an old aquarium, which will stay on Julia's back porch.

The friends have two problems. Will the eggs, which look like little black dots, hatch? And will Julia's little brother Kenny make trouble? He gets into everything. Will he wreck the project?

Patrick has a big family, so he is used to dealing with little brothers. Speaking **solemnly***, as if he's sharing important information, Patrick gives Kenny a task. Since Kenny gets home early from school, would he check the porch thermometer every day? Julia, the narrator of the story, is surprised that Kenny seems willing to do this.*

Kenny nodded. His face was very serious. "I won't forget. I'll check every day, I promise."

I said, "Don't you ever try to move the aquarium yourself. It's way too heavy for you."

Patrick flapped his hand impatiently. "Jules, don't worry about that. Kenny wouldn't do anything to hurt them."

Had Patrick lost his mind? Had he forgotten the millions of times we'd had to redo something Kenny had ruined?

"Yeah, Julia. I'm not *stupid*, you know," Kenny said. He shook his head and looked at Patrick like they were buddies—the two of them against me.

"Thanks, pal," said Patrick. "We're counting on you."

Kenny grinned. Then he said, "I could write it down every day. What the temperature is when I get home. That way you could tell by looking at the numbers if it's getting colder."

What a dumb idea. Like there was no such thing as the Weather Channel.

"That's a great idea!" Patrick said. "Why don't you go and get a pad and pencil, and we'll keep them right here on the porch for you to use."

Kenny disappeared into the house on his **mission** . I could hardly wait until the door closed behind him.

But Patrick rushed right in before I could say anything. "Jules, trust me, this will work. If he feels like he's part of the project, he won't wreck it. Besides, I've been keeping my stuff here for ages, and he never bothers it. He only messes with *your* stuff—that's why I wanted him to feel like it was him and me together on this."

Date   Temperature

LOOK IT UP

For more on insects as pets: raising silkworms, raising butterflies, arthropods as pets, Chinese cricket cages, worm composting, vermiculture, ant farming

I didn't say anything at first. I was thinking. **Reverse psychology**, that's what it was. Patrick was using reverse psychology on Kenny. To keep him away from the project, we'd let him get close to it.

Scary. Because if it didn't work . . .

"Okay," I said at last. "I trust you fine. It's *him* I don't trust. If you're sure this will work—I just hope we don't **regret** it." Then I thought of something else. "Patrick, how come you don't do this kind of thing with *your* little brothers? I mean, it's like you've given up at your house—you just bring everything over here."

Patrick sighed. "It's different when there are three of them," he said. "I'm just way too outnumbered. Besides, it's weird with little brothers—I guess it's easier to be nice to someone else's."

Mulberry leaves and mulberries

• •

Patrick tied the pencil and pad together and hung them from a nail on the wall. The string was long so Kenny could reach them easily. "I'm gonna get started right away," Kenny said. He stared at the thermometer hard, then said, "Sixty-one. It's sixty-one degrees today." He wrote it down and held out the pad so Patrick could see it.

"Good job," Patrick said. "Okay, we're done for today."

We went inside. Patrick got out the **brochure** again. "Six to twenty days," he said. "That's what it says—our eggs will hatch sometime from six to twenty days after we get them."

Twenty days! That was nearly three weeks! "I hope it's six," I said.

It wasn't, of course.

I checked the eggs at least four times a day. When I got up in the morning. When I got home from school. After dinner. Before bed. And sometimes in between those times as well.

Nothing was happening. The eggs looked exactly the same as when we'd first gotten them—gray with a tiny black dot inside. The dots looked like periods.

Patrick had been videotaping every day, but on day six he stopped. "All the tape so far will look exactly the same," he said. "I'm gonna wait until something happens before I film again."

Kenny's numbers already filled up the first few pages of the little pad because he wrote so big. By day eleven, there was still no change in the eggs. "Maybe they're **duds**," I said to Patrick. "Maybe we should write to the **company** and tell them."

Patrick looked worried, too, but he shook his head. "Not yet, Jules. We have to wait until at least day twenty-one."

On day fifteen, Kenny was waiting for us on the front walk again.

"You guys—come see!" he **screeched**.

We dropped our backpacks at the door and pounded through the house to the back porch.

When I first looked, everything seemed the same. Glass dish. Three leaves. No worms.

But then I looked closer.

The little black periods had changed into commas.

"See? See?" Kenny said. "They look different, don't they?"

"They sure do," Patrick said. He grinned at me and then chucked Kenny on top of his head. "Good job, kid." Kenny grinned back at him. "Time to film them."

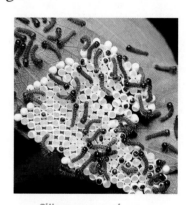

Silkworms and eggs

STOP AND THINK

1. How do the eggs surprise Julia in the end?

2. How does knowing when something is supposed to happen make waiting harder?

UNIT 3
LOOK TO THE SKY

THE BIG QUESTION:

WHY DO PEOPLE LOOK TO THE SKY AND WONDER?

READINGS

Look up at the sky. What can you see?

When I look at the sky, I can see...

☐ the Sun.

☐ the Moon.

☐ the stars.

☐ clouds.

☐ birds.

☐ airplanes.

Which is the largest body in our solar system?

The largest body is...

☐ the Sun.

☐ the Moon.

☐ the Earth.

☐ the clouds.

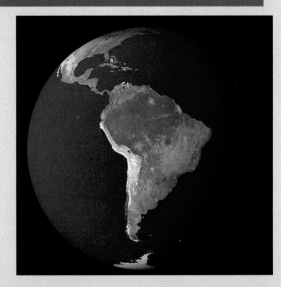

How many full-sized planets are in our solar system?

Our solar system has...

☐ one planet only—
the planet Earth.

☐ two planets.

☐ eight planets.

☐ so many planets that
no one knows the number.

Which object in the sky appears to move, but doesn't?

The object that appears to move, but doesn't, is...

☐ the Sun.

☐ the Moon.

☐ the stars.

Which object appears to change shape, but doesn't?

The object that appears to change shape, but doesn't, is...

☐ the Sun.

☐ the Moon.

☐ the stars.

☐ Earth.

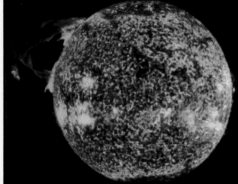

Science Words

atmosphere

crater

crescent

cycle

gravity

lunar

orbit

phase

planet

revolve

atmosphere

Atmosphere is the gases, including air, surrounding Earth or other planets.

66 Without an atmosphere, there would be no life on Earth. 99

crater

A **crater** is a bowl-shaped cavity or dent.

66 The Moon's surface has many large craters. 99

lunar

Lunar means relating to or referring to the Moon.

66 The lunar surface is the surface of the Moon. 99

orbit

To **orbit** means to travel in a path around a larger body.

66 The planets orbit the Sun. 99

crescent

A **crescent** is a narrow or thin curved shape that comes to a point at each end.

66 A crescent moon appears to be much thinner than a full moon. 99

cycle

A **cycle** is a series of events that repeat regularly in the same order.

66 Day following night again and again is an example of a cycle. 99

gravity

Gravity is a force that pulls objects toward each other.

66 Earth's gravity holds the Moon in its orbit around Earth. 99

planet

A **planet** is a large body in space that moves around a star.

66 We live on the planet Earth. 99

phase

A **phase** is a stage of change or development in a cycle.

66 Night is one phase of the day-night cycle. 99

revolve

The word **revolve** means to turn around or rotate in a circular orbit.

66 The Moon revolves around Earth. 99

THE SOLAR SYSTEM

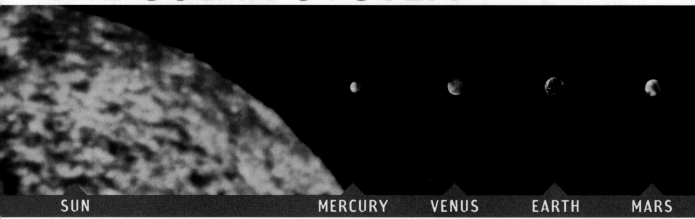

SUN   MERCURY   VENUS   EARTH   MARS

Planet Data

Planet:	Diameter:	Distance from Sun:	Length of Year:
Mercury	4,879 km	57,909,175 km	88 Earth days
Venus	12,104 km	108,208,930 km	225 Earth days
Earth	12,756 km	149,597,890 km	365 Earth days
Mars	9,796 km	227,936,640 km	687 Earth days
Jupiter	142,984 km	778,412,020 km	4,331 Earth days
Saturn	120,536 km	1,426,725,400 km	10,756 Earth days
Uranus	51,118 km	2,870,972,200 km	30,687 Earth days
Neptune	49,528 km	4,498,252,900 km	60,190 Earth days

The Amazing Disappearing Planet

When your parents were children, they learned that there were nine **planets**. From its discovery in 1930 until August 24, 2006, Pluto was the ninth planet in our solar system. Then, scientists decided that Pluto was not a planet. They said that it was a dwarf planet. And Pluto is not even the largest dwarf planet. Eris has that honor.

60

JUPITER   SATURN   URANUS   NEPTUNE

The Sun

The Sun is the star that is the center of our solar system. Earth and all the other planets **revolve** around the Sun. So although it looks like the Sun is moving, it is really the Earth that is moving. The Sun is by far the largest object in our solar system. In fact, if the Sun were hollow, about a million Earths could fit inside.

Moons in Our Solar System

Planet	Number of Moons
Mercury	0
Venus	0
Earth	1
Mars	2
Jupiter	62
Saturn	59
Uranus	27
Neptune	13

Our Solar System

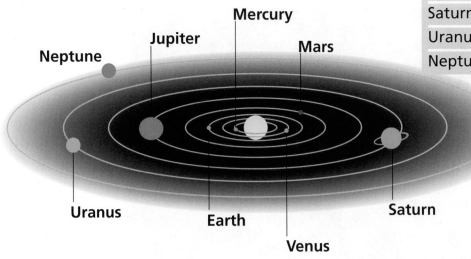

Neptune

Jupiter

Mercury

Mars

Uranus

Earth

Venus

Saturn

61

Comprehension

✔ **TARGET SKILL** **Cause and Effect** When you read about why an event happens, you are reading about cause and effect. The **cause** is **why** something happens. The **effect** is **what happens** as a result of the cause.

Here are two examples of cause and effect:

The Moon is a natural satellite. That means it is a body that is in orbit. The Moon revolves, or moves around, planet Earth. **cause** Earth's gravity pulls the Moon toward our planet. **Therefore, effect** the Moon doesn't float away into space. If gravity pulls the Moon toward Earth, are we in danger? Will the Moon hit us at some time? The answer is *no*. The movement of the Moon tugs **cause** against the pull of Earth's gravity. **As a result,** the Moon keeps **effect** its distance from Earth. Together, the movement of the Moon and Earth's gravity hold the Moon in place.

You can show cause and effect with a graphic organizer.

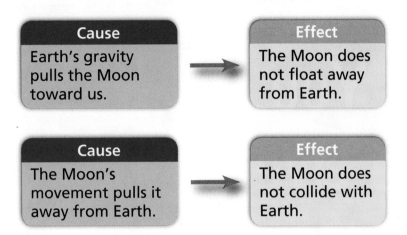

Cause		Effect
Earth's gravity pulls the Moon toward us.	→	The Moon does not float away from Earth.

Cause		Effect
The Moon's movement pulls it away from Earth.	→	The Moon does not collide with Earth.

Notice how the writer uses the signal words *therefore* and *as a result* to help you link cause and effect. Other signal words include *because*, *since*, and *so*.

Signal Words

therefore
as a result
because
since
so

✔ **TARGET STRATEGY** **Ask Questions** As you read, it's important to ask yourself:

• What happens?
• Why does it happen?

These questions will help you uncover cause and effect.

Would You Like to Live on the Moon?

A view of Earth from the Moon

FOCUS: The Moon looks so shiny and inviting when we look to the sky, but what is it really like?

Think twice before you answer that! What do you think you know about the Moon? Can you really say what shape it is? Look for the Moon in the dark sky. Sometimes it looks like a big, round ball, or **sphere**. We say, "Did you see that full Moon tonight?" At times, it looks like a thin slice of pale melon, or a **crescent**. And sometimes we do not see it at all. When the Moon is in that **phase** of its **lunar cycle**, we call it a "new Moon." The Moon appears to change its shape.

The Moon is the brightest object in our night sky. The Moon seems to glow, but it cannot make light all on its own. The Moon **reflects** the Sun's light. What we see is sunlight bouncing off the **surface** of the Moon.

What is the Moon?

The Moon is a natural **satellite**. That means it is a body that is in **orbit**. The Moon revolves, or moves around, planet Earth. Earth's **gravity** pulls the Moon toward our planet. Therefore, the Moon does not float away into space. If gravity pulls the Moon toward Earth, are we in danger? Will the Moon hit us at some time? The answer is *no*. The movement of the Moon tugs against the pull of Earth's gravity. As a result, the Moon keeps its distance from Earth. Together, the movement of the Moon and Earth's gravity hold the Moon in place.

How does the Moon look up close?

The Moon looks bright and shiny from down here. It does not look like that up close. Up close, it looks rather plain and boring. There is no life on the Moon. Plants and animals cannot survive. It is all a dull, pale brown color. Rocks and dust are everywhere.

Look closely at the Moon. You can see big, dark **patches** on its surface. People used to think these dark patches were big seas or oceans. Later, scientists found that they are areas that used to be covered with **lava**. That lava is now hard rock.

satellite Any object that revolves around a planet or other larger object.
lava Very hot, melted rock.

What are craters?

The surface of the Moon is covered with **craters**. These craters were formed long ago. Big and small **asteroids collided** with the Moon. This made craters. An asteroid is a rock that orbits the sun. Craters on the Moon can be tiny or huge. The biggest one is the Aitken Basin. It is 1,398 miles across.

When asteroids collided with the Moon, they crushed lots of rock. This made lots of dust. A fine, powdery dust now lies all over the Moon.

The Moon has valleys and mountains. Its tallest peak is 19,685 feet high.

The Moon has big rocks.

asteroid A piece of rock in space.

What would it feel like to be on the Moon?

So, we have craters, we have mountains, and we have "seas" of old lava. Other than these things, there is not much to see on the Moon. There are no green trees. There is no grass. The Moon is not like Earth. Walking on the Moon is not at all like walking on Earth.

Man steps on the Moon's surface.

Earth has blue skies.

Have you ever seen pictures of astronauts jumping around slowly on the Moon? This is due to its low gravity. The Moon is much smaller than Earth. It has six times less gravity. It is easy to make a big, long jump on the Moon. You cannot make that same jump back here on Earth. Something that is 60 pounds here on Earth is about 10 pounds on the Moon. You would not **struggle** with a heavy backpack!

The Moon has long days and long nights. On Earth, it takes 24 hours for a day and a night to go by. It takes about 29 Earth days for the Moon to have a day and a night.

Does the Moon have an atmosphere?

Earth has a thick blanket of gas around it. This blanket is called the **atmosphere**. The Moon does not have enough gravity to hold an atmosphere around itself. Without an atmosphere, the Moon is different from Earth in many ways. The sky always looks black on the Moon. It can be day or it can be night—it always looks the same. Here on Earth, the sky looks blue when it is day. This is because the sun is shining through its atmosphere. Also, without an atmosphere or air, there is no sound on the Moon. If a person came up behind you and shouted, you would not hear it.

On the Moon a footprint stays the same.

How hot is hot?

So, the Moon has no atmosphere. This means it has no weather. It has no storms, no wind, no rain, no snow, no fog, no sleet, no hail, and no mist. Without weather, the Moon's surface always stays the same. Footprints made by astronauts who walk on the Moon will stay unchanged for a long time.

Earth's atmosphere acts like a blanket. It keeps it from getting too hot or too cold. With no atmosphere, the Moon can be colder and hotter than it ever can be on Earth. When it is daytime the Moon is about 266 degrees. That is a hot day! At night it falls to 290 degrees below zero. With no atmosphere, there is no air to breathe on the Moon. Astronauts who visit the Moon must have on spacesuits. These spacesuits supply them with air to breathe. They also keep astronauts safe from too much heat or too much cold.

Does the Moon sound like a place you would like to live? Use your **imagination** and think about it. The day may come when you can live there. Will you be ready? Pack a big bag!

STOP AND THINK

1. What are some of the ways that living on the Moon would be different from living on Earth?

2. Would you like to live on the Moon? Why or why not?

Astronauts fly to the Moon.

LOOK IT UP

For more on the moon: lunar atlas, moon phases, lunar exploration, Neil Armstrong, Extraterrestrial real estate

Your Turn

Use Your Words:

collide	reflects
drifting	soar
escape	sphere
imagination	struggle
launch	surface
order	waning
patches	waxing
powerful	

I like the way the <u>surface</u> of the water <u>reflects</u> the <u>patches</u> of light.

- Read the words on the list.
- Read the dialogue. Find the words.

MORE ACTIVITIES

1. Make a Venn Diagram
Graphic Organizer
What do you see in the sky that you can only see at night? What do you see in the sky that you could also see during the day? What can you see both day and night?

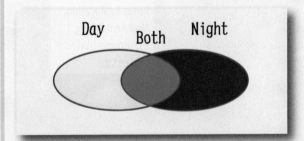

2. Dialogue
Listening and Speaking
Have you seen fireworks? What patterns and designs did you see? Draw them and share them with your partner.

3. You Are the Author
Writing
Use your imagination. Write a poem about anything that is in the sky.

4. Play "Guess It"
Listening and Speaking

One player thinks of something that can be seen in the sky. The other player asks up to five yes-or-no questions to try to figure out what it is.

5. Activities in a Park
Writing

What are your favorite activities in a park? List your top two. Explain your reasons.

6. Make a List
Vocabulary

Make a list of all the surfaces you know that can reflect. Share your list with the class.

Surfaces That Reflect	
In the Drawing	In the Classroom

CULTURAL CONNECTION

INCAS at MACHU PICCHU

Peru

FOCUS: How do we know that the Incas were able to see patterns when they looked to the sky?

Welcome to Machu Picchu! This city is high in the Andes in Peru. It was built more than 500 years ago by the Incas. Inca workers had only the simplest hand tools. Yet they put up huge stone buildings. In Machu Picchu, you will find homes. You will find storehouses for food. There are also temples to the Inca gods. Use your imagination. You can picture the city as it was when people lived here.

The Incas were not just great builders. They also studied the stars. The mountaintop city of Machu Picchu was probably built, in part, for studying the sky and the stars. In Machu Picchu, you can visit a stone called the Intihuatana. It was named for the Sun god, Inti, the most important god of the Incas.

🖥 LOOK IT UP

For more on ancient astronomy: Mayan astronomers, Babylonian astronomers, ancient Greek astronomy, ancient Egyptian astronomy

At noon on two days every year, the Sun is directly over the stone, so the stone casts no shadow. This happens on the two days in the year when day and night are of equal length. These days are the year's two equinoxes. On our calendar, one of the equinoxes is around March 21. The other is around September 21. Our scientists know about the equinoxes by using **powerful** telescopes and other tools. The Incas figured out the equinoxes without such tools.

Intihuatana Stone

Long ago, on the day of each equinox, the Incas held celebrations at Machu Picchu. The Incas believed that these celebrations linked the Sun to Earth. They kept the Sun from **drifting** away.

STOP AND THINK

1. Why is Machu Picchu a good place to study the sky?

2. What happens to the stone on just two days each year?

new Moon

waxing crescent Moon

first-quarter Moon

waxing gibbous Moon

Does the Moon Really Change Shape?

FOCUS: Why does the shape of the Moon change every night when we look to the sky?

What shape is the Moon? Sometimes, the Moon seems to have a shape like a circle or a ball. Sometimes, it looks like the letter "D" or "C." Sometimes, it looks like a backward "D" or "C." It all depends on the day you look at the Moon.

It is the Sun that lights the Moon. The Moon does not make its own light. It reflects light from the Sun, like a mirror. We see the Moon when sunlight bounces off the surface of the Moon.

The Moon revolves around our planet, Earth. It moves on a path around the Earth. It stays on that path at all times. Each day, as the Moon revolves, we see a different part of the Moon that is lit by the Sun. The shapes we can see are called the phases of the Moon.

REREAD

Cause ➡ Effect

Why is a different part of the Moon lit each day?

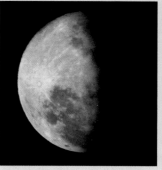

| full Moon | waning gibbous Moon | last-quarter Moon | waning crescent Moon |

New Moon

As this phase begins, the Moon is between Earth and the Sun. We can't see any Moon at all. This is called a new Moon.

Full Moon

Sometimes the Moon is behind Earth. It is not blocked by Earth's shadow. We see one whole side of the Moon. This is called a full Moon. As the Moon moves around Earth, we can see different parts of it. We see the parts that the Sun lights up. The Moon's phases are pictured above.

REREAD

Cause → Effect

Why do we sometimes see one whole side of the Moon?

The Lunar Cycle

The full trip of the Moon around Earth is called a cycle. *Lunar* is an adjective that means "moon." In one lunar cycle, we see all the phases of the Moon. The phases happen in the same **order**. The full cycle of Moon phases takes $29\frac{1}{2}$ days to complete. That is, it takes $29\frac{1}{2}$ days to go from the start of the new Moon to the end of the waning crescent Moon. One cycle of $29\frac{1}{2}$ days is a lunar month. In about one month, we can see all six phases of the Moon.

If you know the phases of the Moon, you can predict when the next full Moon will come.

STOP AND THINK

1. Why does the Moon appear to change shape?

2. Sometimes, even on clear nights, we can't see the Moon. Why is that?

....
gibbous More than half, but less than full.

Apollo 11 Astronauts Land on Moon
Moon Walk Safely Completed

▲ The astronauts left scientific equipment behind on the moon.

FOCUS: What happens when just looking at the sky is not enough?

HOUSTON, TX, JULY 20, 1969 — "The Eagle has landed." At 4:17 P.M., Eastern Daylight Time, *Apollo 11*'s lunar module *Eagle* landed on the Moon. Then astronaut Neil Armstrong spoke those words. Six hours later, he became the first person ever to walk on the Moon.

The *Apollo 11* mission began four days ago, on July 16th. The world watched as NASA's powerful Saturn rocket **launched** three men into space. The rocket quickly **soared** through the atmosphere. It **escaped** from Earth's gravity. It took three days to reach the Moon. Once in orbit around the Moon, *Apollo* split into two parts. The command module with astronaut Michael Collins stayed in orbit. The lunar module traveled down to the Moon. Neil Armstrong and Buzz Aldrin were in the module.

▲ Astronaut Neil Armstrong landed the lunar module safely.

First Steps on the Moon

It took Armstrong and Aldrin more than six hours to get ready to leave the module. Armstrong had to squeeze through the hatch door. It was hard because of his large spacesuit and equipment. When he stepped onto the Moon itself, he said words that will become famous.

"That's one small step for a man, one giant leap for mankind."

At Work on the Moon

Armstrong and Aldrin spent more than two hours on the Moon's surface. They took pictures. They set up experiments. They collected Moon rocks. Armstrong talked about the surface of the Moon. "The surface is fine and powdery.... I only go in a fraction of an inch.... But I can see the footprints of my boots."

Heading Home

The astronauts have gone back to the lunar module, where they will complete their work. They will take off from the Moon in the next few hours. Then they plan to meet up with Collins in the command module. The three *Apollo* astronauts will be heading home sometime later today. The return journey is expected to take about three days.

A **plaque** and an American flag will be left on the Moon. The plaque reads: "Here men from the planet Earth first set foot upon the Moon, July 1969, A.D. We came in peace for all mankind."

....
plaque A metal sign.

■■■ STOP AND THINK

1. Why did the *Apollo* split into two pieces?
2. Why did Armstrong call the Moon landing a "giant leap"?
3. Why do you think the *Apollo 11* astronauts left a plaque on the Moon?

Two poets look to the Moon and wonder . . .

The Moon's the North Wind's Cookie

The Moon's the North Wind's cookie.
He bites it, day by day,
Until there's but a rim of **scraps**
That crumble all away.

The South Wind is a baker.
He kneads clouds in his **den**,
And bakes a crisp new moon that . . . *greedy*
. . . North . . . Wind . . . eats . . . again!

—*Vachel Lindsay*

Vachel Lindsay (1879–1931)

Lindsay was born in his family's home in Springfield, Illinois. He died there 52 years later. Lindsay was a poet and an artist. To share his poems and his art with others, he made three long trips on foot. In all, Lindsay walked 2,800 miles across America! Along the way, he sold his poems and his art for food and lodging.

scraps Small bits or little pieces of something.
den Home.

FULL MOON

Night on the **verandah:**
Across the bay
Village lights
Sprinkled on hills
Stripe the dark water

The silver round
Of the full moon
Slips into the cloud
As a coin
Slips into a purse

—*Ashley Bryan*

Ashley Bryan (Born: 1923)

Bryan grew up in Harlem. He made his first book when he was in kindergarten. He is well known both as an author and as an illustrator. In his work he has explored the African American experience, looking at oral traditions. His travels in Africa inspired him to retell and illustrate traditional African folktales. Bryan now lives on an island off the coast of Maine.

verandah An open porch.

UNIT 4

SHOW ME THE MONEY!

LOOK AT MONEY

Before there was money, what did people use to buy or trade?

Before there was money, people used...

- ☐ salt to buy or trade.
- ☐ shells to buy or trade.
- ☐ cattle to buy or trade.
- ☐ seeds to buy or trade.

How can you make your money grow?

You can make your money grow by...

- ☐ putting it under your mattress.
- ☐ having a savings account.
- ☐ buying stocks.
- ☐ buying collectibles.

What collectibles can increase in value?

Collectibles that can increase in value are...

☐ coins.

☐ stamps.

☐ comic books.

☐ baseball cards.

What happens to the price of a product when there is a big demand for it?

When there is a big demand for a product, the price...

☐ goes down.

☐ stays the same.

☐ goes up.

☐ doubles.

In what ways is a dollar valuable?

A dollar is valuable because you can...

☐ trade it for gold.

☐ buy something with it.

☐ pay a debt with it.

☐ frame it.

LEARN THE WORDS

Economics Words

- brief
- crude
- demand
- desire
- electronic
- issue
- shortage
- steady
- strain
- striking

---

brief

Brief means lasting only a short period of time.

> 66 It was a brief meeting, so we were done in a few minutes. 99

crude

Crude means rough, not well finished.

> 66 Maya's first painting was crude, but she soon became more skillful. 99

issue

To **issue** means to give out, distribute, or publish something.

> 66 The store will issue discount coupons soon. 99

shortage

A **shortage** means less of something than is needed.

> 66 There was a shortage of sandwiches, so we had to share. 99

demand

Demand is the wish to own a particular item.

66 There was a great demand for the sneakers because every kid in school wanted a pair. 99

desire

To **desire** is to wish for something.

66 Gene desired a new bike so strongly that he got a job to pay for it. 99

electronic

Electronic is a word that describes devices and systems that are controlled by a computer.

66 An electronic collar kept track of the dog's location. 99

steady

Steady is in an even and regular manner, without variation.

66 The snow fell at a steady rate of about an inch an hour. 99

strain

Strain means stress that goes beyond the proper limit.

66 The high cost of heating oil put a strain on the family budget, forcing them to cut back on their spending. 99

striking

Striking means very impressive and hard to ignore.

66 The painting was striking, and everyone who saw it fell in love with it. 99

THE $TORY OF MONEY

FROM CATTLE TO CREDIT

9000-6000 B.C.E.

Salt, tea, cattle, and seeds are the first forms of money. In farming societies, they are easy to trade.

5000-1200 B.C.E.

Shells are used as money. Cowrie shells are used in Africa and Asia. Wampum, strands of shell beads, are used in North America.

2500 B.C.E.

Gold bars and gold rings are first traded in Egypt. Gold becomes a popular item to trade in many countries. Gold has value. It can be worn.

1000-500 B.C.E.

The first **crude** coins appear in China. They are made from cheap metal. The coins are stamped to show their worth. Gold coins are first used in Turkey.

CATTLE WERE ONCE USED AS MONEY.

Money makes the world go around, or so it is said. But bills and coins have not always existed.

Before there was money, people traded goods and services. A farmer might trade a sack of wheat for some lumber. A merchant might trade a bolt of cloth for some salt. But what if you couldn't agree on how much salt someone's cloth was worth? What if another person didn't want what you had to trade? What if you didn't want to carry around a bag of wheat? Money solved these problems.

CREDIT CARD

650–800 C.E.
During a copper **shortage**, paper money appears **briefly** in China.

1950s
The first credit cards are **issued** in the United States. They are made by Diner's Club.

1960s
The first ATM (automated teller machine) is installed in England. People can withdraw money from a machine.

TODAY
Electronic banking is used worldwide. You may never see your paycheck.

CHINESE COIN

Comprehension

✔ **TARGET SKILL** **Problem/Solution** In an informational article, a writer may tell about problems and how the problems are solved. Sometimes one problem will have several solutions. Other times two or more problems will have the same solution.

Here is an example of two problems that have the same solution:

Coins used to be worth their weight in gold or silver. Paper money, too, used to be "good as gold." You could take your paper bills straight to a bank and trade them for gold or silver.

Over time, more and more people were born. The economy grew. The United States needed more money so that everyone could keep buying things. The demand for gold grew. This put a strain on the supply of gold. By 1971, gold mines could no longer keep up with demand. So the United States stopped trading dollars for gold. It declared that dollars were still worth 100 cents—but their value was no longer backed up by gold.

Problem 1

Problem 2

Solution

The signal word *So* tells you that the information in the sentence is a solution.

Problem 1

The growing demand for gold put a strain on the supply of gold.

Problem 2

Eventually, gold mines could not supply the amount of gold needed.

Solution

The United States stopped trading dollars for gold.

Each box on the left shows a problem. The box on the right shows the solution. Notice that an arrow from each box on the left points to the solution box on the right. This shows that the two problems had the same solution.

✓ TARGET STRATEGY **Analyze/Evaluate** As you read, you can use a graphic organizer like the one above to help you analyze problems and solutions in an article.

To evaluate the way problems and solutions are presented, you can ask yourself questions such as the following:

• Does the writer use signal words such as *so* and *as a result* to help me identify problems and solutions?

• Is a solution presented for each problem, or do some problems remain unsolved?

CASH:
As Good as
GOLD...
Or is it?

FOCUS: What gives money its buying power?

Gold bars

Why does cash have value? This may surprise you. You may even scream when you find out that the paper and metal in your pocket has little value at all. It sounds a little strange, but it's true. Dollars and cents are just slips of paper and metal disks. The paper and metal aren't valuable. But the dollars and cents are.

Most things that people value have a use. A coat keeps you warm. A car gets you around. But a dollar bill is no more useful than any other piece of paper, except that you can spend this one.

Coins used to be worth their weight in gold or silver. Paper money, too, used to be "good as gold." You could take your paper bills straight to a bank and trade them for gold or silver.

Over time, more and more people were born. The economy grew. The United States needed more money so that everyone could keep buying things. The **demand** for gold grew. This put a **strain** on the supply of gold. By 1971, gold mines could no longer keep up with demand. So the United States stopped trading dollars for gold. It declared that dollars were still worth 100 cents—but their value was no longer backed up by gold.

> **LOOK IT UP**
>
> For more information on money: history of money, U.S. Mint, African trade beads, currency converter

Since then, dollars have been just pieces of paper. So why do they still have buying power? There is one good reason: faith in our money **system**. The government prints money and declares that it can be used to buy anything we might **desire**. People know they can spend their dollars at the store.

If enough of us lose faith in the **steady** value of our coins and bills, something very **striking** happens. Our economy slows down. Some people worry about this. So they buy as much gold as they can. They think gold is safer than cash. If more people thought the same way, there could be a **panic**. Soon our money would be worth no more than paper.

Experts work hard to prevent this from happening. Their goal is to ensure that money will keep its value. This system has worked for a long time. As long as we spend money—and **strive** to get more of it—the system will keep working. So take good care of those slips of paper and metal disks in your pocket. They're valuable.

STOP AND THINK

1. When did the U.S. government stop backing the value of dollars with gold?

2. Do you think gold is safer than cash? Explain.

LEARN THE WORDS

Your Turn

Use Your Words:

defy	product
inflation	profit
interest	rate
invest	recent
noted	strive
odds	suppose
panic	system
potential	

- Read the words on the list.
- Read the dialogue. Find the words.

The checks have cleared. Your money is available.

I made a <u>recent</u> deposit. What are the <u>odds</u> that the checks have cleared?

MORE ACTIVITIES

1. Take a Survey
Graphic Organizer

Ask twelve classmates how they would invest money. Tally their answers. Share your findings with your class.

How Would You Invest Your Money?		
Stock market	Savings account	Buy collectibles (stamps, comic books, rare coins)

2. Make a List
Vocabulary

With a partner, make a list of all the ways people use money. Share your list with your class.

3. You Are the Author
Writing

Suppose you had $100. Write a paragraph telling how you would use it. Share your paragraph with your partner.

4. Play "Guess It"

Listening and Speaking

One player thinks of something that can be seen in a bank. The other player asks up to five yes-or-no questions to try to figure out what it is.

5. Your Activities

Writing

Some of the activities you do cost money. List five activities. Next to each one write the cost. Compare your list with your partner's list.

6. Dialogue

Listening and Speaking

Suppose you wanted to sell your favorite comic book. Draw a picture of the comic and share it with your partner. Tell your partner why buying the book would be a good investment.

Money
Doesn't
Grow
on
Trees

Suppose you have $100. It would be fun to spend it, but you want to save your money. You want it to grow. What should you do with your $100? You have many choices.

1. You can put your cash under your mattress or in a piggy bank. Those are safe places, right? Not really. Someone could steal the money. But even if no one steals it, the **odds** are that you will lose some money. Why? Over time, the prices of goods and services usually increase. Things you buy next year will cost more than they did last year. This is called **inflation**, and it eats away at the value of cash. As time goes by, your $100 will be worth less and less.

2. You can put your money in a savings account. Your money will be safe in a bank, but it won't grow very fast there. In fact, you may still lose money. How could that be? Remember inflation—prices usually increase over time. A bank will pay you interest, so your money will grow. But if inflation grows faster, you will lose money. At the end of 10 years, you will have more cash, but that cash may be worth less than the $100 you started with.

3. So how can you get ahead? You can **invest** your $100 in stocks or bonds. A bond is a loan. When you buy a bond, you lend your money to a company or to part of the government. After some time goes by, you get your money back, with **interest**. A stock is a share of a company. When you buy a stock, you own a small part of the company. If the company does well, the value of its stock should rise. So your investment grows. There is a catch, though. If the stock loses value, so does your investment.

93

Can you take the risk? If you can, investing in stocks might be a good idea. Your $100 has the **potential** to grow a lot. Suppose you buy stock from Company A and the value of the stock rises 10 percent a year. In a little more than 7 years, your money will double. That sounds great. But remember, you can lose money, too. If Company A's stock loses value, some of the lost value will be yours.

$100 Investment in Company A's Stock
(10 percent growth per year)

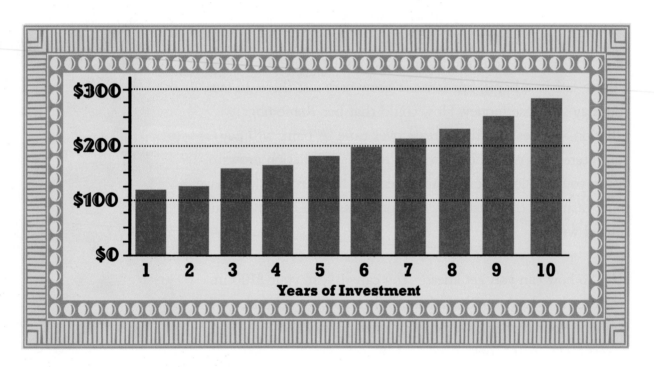

4. You can use your $100 to buy collectibles such as rare coins, stamps, gems, and paintings. Some people buy collectibles as an investment. They hope to sell them later for more than what they paid. But this kind of investment is far from foolproof. The painting you bought could be worth millions of dollars some day in the future. Or it could turn out to be worthless. There goes your $100.

If you need your $100 to live on, you should put it somewhere safe. A savings account would be a good place. But if you can take some risk, you may want to invest that $100. Money can and does grow— but not on trees.

STOP AND THINK

1. What is the disadvantage of putting your money in a savings account?

2. How would you invest $100?

Comics

A SUPERHERO WAY TO EARN

FOCUS: How can comic books be a good investment?

Many people buy coins, stamps, and other collectibles as investments. They think they can sell them at a **profit**. But that's a risky move. Most collectibles don't earn as much as stocks do. But comic books seem to have superhero powers. Between 1937 and 2006, comic-book investors did almost 12 percent better than stock investors.

Early comic books

Collecting stamps and coins can be fun. But over time, most collectibles earn far less than stocks do. Comic books **defy** those odds. Over the past 70 years, many rare comics have leaped way ahead of stocks.

Hey, if you want to invest in comics, think about these facts first.

Stamp album

 Most new comic books are bought by kids who don't take very good care of them. For your comic books to increase in value, they need to be in great shape. Old comic books in near-mint condition can sell for huge sums.

Some people who invest in comics are fans. Comics matter to them. Others are more interested in the money. One man in Texas bought near-mint comics from the early 1940s. "One… increased in value by 18 percent this year," he said. "The others go up between 12 and 18 percent. I can't do that well in the stock market."

LOOK IT UP

For more on profitable collections: collecting coins, collecting stamps, collecting model cars

Marvel Comics #1 from 1939 introduced *The Human Torch*. Ten years ago, it was worth just $42,000. It **recently** went for $350,000.

DC Comics published the first *Batman* comic in 1938. It sold for $80,000 in 1992. It is now worth $300,000. The stock of Time Warner, which owns DC Comics, has grown only about half that much since 1992.

Comics are some of today's best moneymakers. Go ahead and collect them for fun. But don't bank on comics to make you millions. Collecting is always risky. Most experts still think stocks are the surest way to get ahead.

STOP AND THINK

1. How does the condition of old comic books affect their value?

2. What could you collect now that might increase in value in the future?

JEANS, PRICES, AND INFLATION

FOCUS: How are prices set and why do they change?

Maya Johnson: Hello, Mr. Fenton, and thank you for giving me this interview. The students of Greenfield School will be glad to learn about prices from a **noted** economist.

Edward Fenton: It's my pleasure, Maya. I hope I can answer your questions clearly. We economists are not known for plain speech.

MJ: My first question is basic: how do companies set prices?

EF: Let's consider an imaginary blue jeans company. Let's call it Blue Sky. How does Blue Sky put a price on the jeans it makes?

Each pair of jeans costs a certain amount to produce and sell. The company has to design the jeans. It has to buy fabric. It has to pay someone to sew the jeans. It has to ship the jeans to stores. Finally, it has to advertise the jeans. All these things cost money. Maybe it costs Blue Sky a total of $10 to make each pair of jeans. The company needs to charge more than $10 to make a profit. So maybe it charges $15. Then it will earn $5 profit on each pair it sells.

REREAD

Problem/Solution

What problem does the company have? What is the solution?

98

MJ: Why do prices change sometimes?

EF: Prices can change for all sorts of reasons. The cost of making a **product** can go up or down. Suppose bad weather causes cotton crops to do poorly. There will be less cotton for sale, so its price will increase. Because Blue Sky's jeans are made from cotton, their production costs increase. And their prices will rise, too.

Another reason prices change is that demand changes. If Blue Sky's jeans become a must-have item for teens, demand for the jeans will grow. Stores will notice, and Blue Sky will notice. Since everyone wants to own a pair of these popular jeans, the company will be able to charge more. When demand for a product is high, prices may rise.

Now suppose Blue Sky decides to make more jeans to meet demand. What happens when Blue Sky's jeans are no longer the rage? Fewer people want to buy the jeans. Stores might have too many of the jeans in stock. To sell the jeans, stores will need to lower the price. So when the supply of a product is high, prices may go down.

> **REREAD**
>
> **Problem/Solution**
>
> How do stores solve the problem of having too many jeans in stock?

99

We also have to consider the value of money itself. Today, a dollar isn't worth as much as a dollar ten years ago. Today's dollar won't buy as much. Over time, companies and stores adjust their prices—upward. When prices increase across the economy, we call it inflation.

MJ: Oh, so that's what inflation is. How long has the value of the dollar been changing?

EF: It's always changing. The government keeps track of the prices of goods and services that people buy. That gives us an idea of the **rate** of inflation. And it tells us how the value of the dollar is changing. Look at this graph I made. In 2007, it took $21 to buy what $1 bought in 1913.

MJ: Well, what causes inflation?

THE VALUE OF ONE 1913 DOLLAR

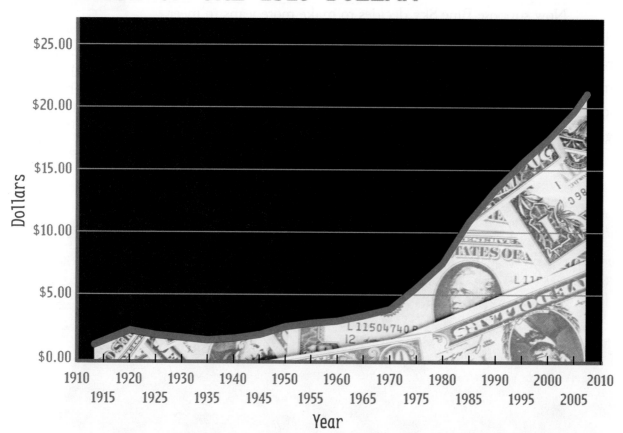

EF: That's a hard question to answer. Economists argue about inflation a lot. Different things cause inflation at different times. If the government greatly increases its spending, say during a war, that can cause inflation. More money is being spent. But companies can't increase their production fast enough. So prices go up.

Sometimes inflation is caused by price increases in a single industry. Think about the oil industry. Companies need oil to run their factories. Cities need oil to run their power plants. People need oil to heat their homes and gasoline to run their cars. If the price of oil rises enough, a lot of other prices will rise, too. There's some inflation.

And many economists think inflation can be caused by expectations. Let's say that the inflation rate last year was three percent. And let's say it was three percent the year before. Companies and stores probably expect inflation this year to be three percent. So everybody raises prices three percent. That's inflation, too.

MJ: Thanks very much, Mr. Fenton. I'm sure all the students at Greenfield School will enjoy learning about prices and inflation.

STOP AND THINK

1. What is inflation?

2. What do you know that costs more today than it did last year?

LITERATURE CONNECTION

A SPIN *on the* USUAL STORY

FOCUS: How can Rumpelstiltskin save the miller's daughter?

One day on the road, by chance, a poor miller met the king. To make himself seem important, the miller told the king, "My daughter can spin straw into gold!"

The king's eyes lit up, for he loved gold. "Send her to my palace," he said. "She sounds like a clever girl indeed!"

When the girl arrived, the king barely said hello. He led her to a room full of straw. "Spin this straw into gold by morning or die," he said, and left. Of course, the poor miller's daughter could not spin straw into gold. She began to weep.

Like magic, a little man appeared. "Why are you crying?" The girl explained her situation. The little man said he would help, but only if she could make him laugh. She told her favorite joke. The little man giggled. He chuckled and chortled. Finally, he laughed till he cried. This cheered the girl up considerably. The little man sat at the spinning wheel and worked until all the straw was gone, replaced by gleaming gold. He vanished before she could thank him.

At dawn, the king returned. He crowed with delight when he saw the gold. Taking the girl to a bigger room with more straw, he said, "Spin gold or die." Again the girl cried. Again the little man appeared. Again the girl made him laugh, and he spun straw into gold. And again he vanished mysteriously.

The king jumped for joy. He took the girl to a giant cellar full of straw. "Spin gold or die," he commanded. For the third time, the girl wept, the little man appeared, she made him laugh, he spun straw into gold, and then he disappeared.

The greedy king was now madly in love… with his new piles of gold. Perhaps he should keep this girl around, he thought. So he bowed down and proposed marriage to the miller's daughter.

"Um…can I sleep on it?" she asked. The king was furious at her reply. He slammed the cellar door shut, locking her in for the night. She began to cry, and once more the little man appeared. There was no straw, so he was quite puzzled. The girl explained. "The king thinks I spun those piles of gold. Now he wants to marry me! Please help me." The two thought of a plan.

When the king returned in the morning, the miller's daughter was nowhere in sight, but the little man stepped out to greet him. "Rumpelstiltskin is my name," he began, "and it is I who spun the straw into gold, but the—" The angry king lunged to grab him, but Rumpelstiltskin disappeared into thin air.

The miller's daughter came out from her hiding place. She confessed that she could not spin straw into gold at all and that Rumpelstiltskin had helped her. But "Rumpel," as she now called him, could spin gold only after he laughed. And only she could make him laugh.

The king was crestfallen. "Don't worry," she told him. "Rumpel and I are going to start a business together. The taxes alone will keep you in gold." The king knew a good deal when he heard one. So no one married anyone, but Rumpel-Miller, Inc., was born, and they all earned happily ever after.

STOP AND THINK

1. Why did Rumpelstiltskin help the miller's daughter?

2. What joke would you tell Rumpelstiltskin to make him laugh?

UNIT 5 BOLD ADVENTURE

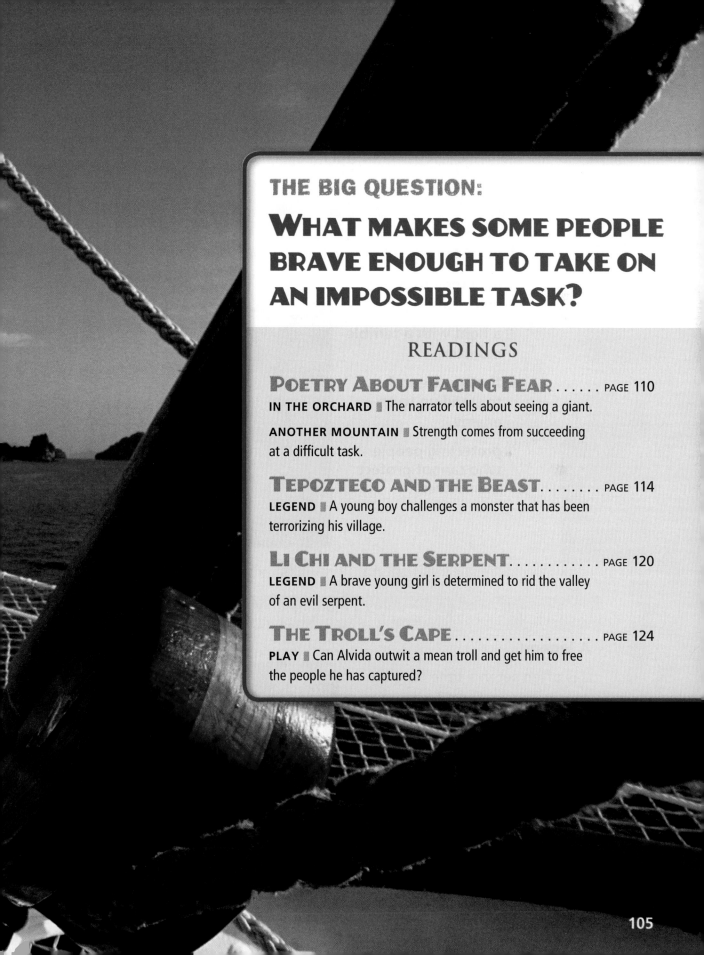

LOOK AT BOLD ADVENTURES

What kinds of things would you consider a bold adventure to be?

I consider a bold adventure to be...

- ☐ a journey to a new and exciting place.

- ☐ a fight with a terrible monster.

- ☐ finding strength to stand up to an enemy.

- ☐ protecting people who cannot protect themselves.

What are some elements of a legend?

A legend...

- ☐ is often set in a time long ago.

- ☐ may tell about unbelievable deeds or events.

- ☐ shows the main character facing a big challenge.

- ☐ features a main character who becomes a hero.

What does it mean to be bold?

To be bold means to...

☐ be brave.

☐ be unafraid.

☐ be strong.

☐ be daring.

What monsters do we find in literature?

Some monsters we find in literature are...

☐ dragons.

☐ serpents.

☐ trolls.

☐ giants.

What are some ways a hero might overcome a monster?

A hero might overcome a monster by...

☐ fighting it.

☐ outwitting it.

☐ making it leave.

☐ taming it.

Literature Words

- argue
- avalanche
- bristle
- dread
- orchard
- plateau
- plunge
- smother
- trample
- weary

argue

Argue means to present reasons for or against a thing.

" She tried to argue that she could kill the monster. "

avalanche

An **avalanche** is snow or rock that tumbles down a mountainside, or an overwhelming amount of something.

" An avalanche of paper fell to the floor from the shelf. "

plateau

A **plateau** is a land area with a level top that is higher than land areas around it.

" From the plateau we could look out over the valley. "

plunge

Plunge means to cast or throw oneself or something into a place or substance—like water.

" She plunged her hand into the icy water to save the dog. "

bristle

Bristle means to act in an angry or unfriendly manner.

❝ The cat bristled when it saw the big dog. ❞

dread

Dread means to fear greatly.

❝ The villagers dreaded passing by the monster's cave. ❞

orchard

An **orchard** is an area of land where fruit trees are grown.

❝ Every fall we pick apples in an apple orchard. ❞

smother

Smother means to cover thickly or suffocate.

❝ We smothered the campfire to make sure it did not start a forest fire. ❞

trample

Trample means to step or stamp heavily and noisily.

❝ The deer trampled Mom's flower bed. ❞

weary

Weary means physically and mentally tired due to hard work.

❝ The farmer was weary after the long day in the fields. ❞

In the ORCHARD

There was a giant by the **Orchard** Wall
Peeping about on this side and on that,
And feeling in the trees. He was as tall
As the big apple tree, and twice as fat:
His beard poked out, all **bristly** -black, and there
Were leaves and gorse and heather in his hair.

He held a blackthorn club in his right hand,
And **plunged** the other into every tree,
Searching for something—You could stand
Beside him and not reach up to his knee,
So big he was—I trembled lest he should
Come **trampling** , round-eyed, down to where I stood.

I tried to get away.—But, as I slid
Under a bush, he saw me, and he bent
Down deep at me, and said, *'Where is she hid?'*
I pointed over there, and off he went—

But, while he searched, I turned and simply flew
Round by the lilac bushes back to you.

—*James Stephens*

ANOTHER MOUNTAIN

Sometimes there's a mountain
that I must climb
even after I've climbed one already
But my legs are tired now
and my arms need a rest
my mind is too **weary** right now
But I must climb before the storm comes
before the earth rocks
and an **avalanche** of clouds buries me
and **smothers** my soul
And so I prepare myself for another climb
Another Mountain
and I tell myself it is nothing
it is just some more dirt and stone
and every now and then I should reach
another **plateau** and enjoy the view
of the trees and the flowers below
And I am young enough to climb
and strong enough to make it to any top
You see the wind has warned me
about settling too long
about peace without struggle
The wind has warned me
and taught me how to fly
But my wings only work
After I've climbed a mountain

—Abiodun Oyewole

Comprehension

✓ **TARGET SKILL** **Inference** You can make inferences about the characters in a story or a play by using story clues. These clues can include the words and actions of the character and the words of the author. Since a play is made up mostly of the characters' speech and actions, you need to be especially alert to understand the characters.

Here is an excerpt from the play "The Troll's Cape." The troll is disguised as a handsome man, because he wants to capture Alvida to work as an unpaid servant in his castle. If she steps on his special cape, she will be unable to escape.

Troll *(to himself):* I'll take that one. *(To Alvida):* Good morning, ma'am. What a lovely day.

Alvida: Yes, isn't it? …

Troll *(spreading his cape on the ground):* A beautiful lady such as you shouldn't have your dainty feet touch the ground.

Alvida *(laughing):* Beautiful? Not me! And you should take better care of that fine cape. Look how it's getting covered with earth and pine needles. *(She picks it up, shakes it out, and hands it to the troll.)* Thank you for your politeness, though.

> The troll's smooth words to Alvida show that he's good at lying and deceiving people.

> Alvida's words and actions show that she is modest about her looks and also helpful to others.

You can use this graphic organizer to keep track of clues from the story and inferences you make.

Clues	Inference
Troll (to himself): I'll take that one. (To Alvida): Good morning, ma'am. What a lovely day.	The troll thinks one thing and says another. His tone of voice is probably different, too.
Troll (spreading his cape on the ground): A beautiful lady such as yourself shouldn't have your dainty feet touch the ground.	He is good at making something up if it suits his purpose. Here, he uses flattery.
Alvida (laughing): Beautiful? Not me!	Alvida's words and her laugh show that flattery isn't something that will work on her.
Alvida: And you should take better care of that fine cape. …(She picks it up, shakes it out, and hands it to the troll.)	Alvida's words and her action show that she is helpful even to strangers.

✔ **TARGET STRATEGY** **Predict** You can use clues from a story and knowledge from your own experience to predict what will happen next in a story. As you read, ask yourself the following questions:

- What do clues in the story tell me about the main character and other characters?
- What do I know from my own experiences about characters like these and stories like these?
- Based on what I can infer about the characters, what do I think will happen in the story?

Think about which clues help you the most to make your prediction.

TEPOZTECO
— and —
THE BEAST

an Aztec tale adapted by Judy Rosenbaum

FOCUS: Why is it important to have stories that tell about brave heroes?

Old tales and legends from all around the world have giants, dragons, serpents, and other dangerous, threatening beings. That's when someone needs to take action. A heroic man or woman often steps forward to meet the challenge. In this Aztec story from ancient Mexico, the evil creature is a huge monster, while the hero is a ten-year-old boy!

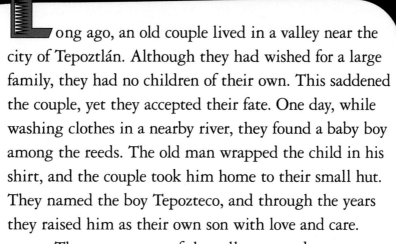

Long ago, an old couple lived in a valley near the city of Tepoztlán. Although they had wished for a large family, they had no children of their own. This saddened the couple, yet they accepted their fate. One day, while washing clothes in a nearby river, they found a baby boy among the reeds. The old man wrapped the child in his shirt, and the couple took him home to their small hut. They named the boy Tepozteco, and through the years they raised him as their own son with love and care.

The eastern part of the valley was a dangerous place, because a **dreadful** monster lived there. This beast terrorized the people of the valley. He hungered for humans. He often demanded that the villagers send him someone, or he'd finish off the whole village. Whenever he made that demand, an older person from the village would be chosen to feed to the beast.

The day came when Tepozteco's own father was chosen as the next victim. "Father," said Tepozteco, "Please, don't go. I'm young and strong and will go in your place."

"No," said his father, "I've lived a long time, while you have your whole life to look forward to. Besides, you're so small. You'd barely make a mouthful for that awful monster. He'd never be satisfied with just you as a meal."

Tepozteco was determined, however. He **argued** and argued until, at last, the old couple agreed to let him go. Before he left, Tepozteco told his parents to watch the eastern skies. If they saw a white cloud of smoke, it would mean he had killed the monster. Then the boy set off for the east.

As he walked along the dusty road toward the monster's cave, Tepozteco picked up pieces of sharp **obsidian** and put them in a **pouch** he was carrying. Before long he found himself at the mouth of the cave. "Come out, beast," he called, "I am your meal for today."

Slowly the monster emerged from the cave. He looked around and finally focused on the young boy in front of him. "How dare the people mock me in such a way!" he **bellowed**. "You are so small I could eat ten of you in one gulp! Go tell the people to send me someone bigger, or else I'll come and destroy them and their village!"

Tepozteco did not move and said nothing. The greedy monster eyed him carefully. He was hungry and didn't want to wait for someone new. In a flash, he snatched up Tepozteco and swallowed him whole.

a piece of obsidian

Tepozteco found himself inside the belly of the beast, alive and whole. He reached into his pouch and pulled out the pieces of sharp, black obsidian he had picked up. Quickly, he began to slice away at the monster's stomach. He worked faster and faster, until he had cut a hole right through the monster's tough skin.

Tepozteco crawled out into the bright sunshine. He saw that the beast lay dead on the ground. He had saved his family and the people of the valley. He built a fire, and a cloud of billowy white smoke filled the eastern sky. His parents and the people of the valley celebrated. They knew that the dreaded monster was dead.

Tepozteco became known far and wide for his **wisdom** and bravery. When he came of age, the people made him king. As a ruler, Tepozteco watched over and protected his people, and no monster **dared** to enter the valley again.

REREAD

Inference

How do you know from this passage that Tepozteco is someone who keeps a promise?

STOP AND THINK

1. In what way did Tepozteco plan ahead for his meeting with the beast?

2. Why might someone volunteer to do something brave?

Your Turn

Use Your Words:

bellow	obsidian
blacksmith	pouch
clench	praise
cloak	province
dainty	reptile
dare	salary
fling	scaly
furious	tiresome
graze	volunteer
mayor	wisdom

- Read the words on the list.
- Read the dialogue. Find the words.

A dragon grazes on the mountainside. That scaly reptile bellows every night.

No one in the province can sleep. It's getting tiresome.

Look, the mayor put up a sign.

MORE ACTIVITIES

1. Take a Survey

Graphic Organizer

Would you volunteer to quiet a bellowing dragon? Ask ten classmates whether they would or would not volunteer. If they answer yes, ask how they plan to do it. Tally the responses and display them in a graph.

Name	Quiet the dragon? Yes or No?	If "yes," how?

2. Make a Wanted Poster

Listening and Speaking

Make a wanted poster for the dragon that bellows. Be sure to include the reward. Show the poster to your partner. Talk about it.

3. Make a List
Vocabulary

Fling means "to throw." *Clench* means "to hold tightly." Think of words that mean the same or almost the same as each of these two words. Make a list and share it with your class.

4. Stop the Bellowing Dragon
Writing

How would you stop the bellowing dragon? Think of a way you could do it. Write about it. Share your idea with your class.

5. Play the Word Game
Speaking and Listening

Play this game with a partner. Think of the word "dainty." What kinds of things can *dainty* describe? Without sharing ideas, each partner writes a list of words that can be described using the word *dainty*. Then Player One says, "A _____ is dainty," filling in one of his or her words. Player Two repeats the sentence, filling in a new word. Play continues until both players run out of words.

LI CHI AND THE SERPENT

A CHINESE TALE
ADAPTED BY
CHRISTINE ECONOMOS

FOCUS: Why might someone who seems small and weak challenge a much stronger enemy?

In this ancient Chinese story, the evil creature is a giant serpent—a kind of reptile. The fighter is a girl who has a simple wish: she doesn't want to be the serpent's breakfast.

Long ago, a terrible serpent came to live in some mountains in the east of China. This serpent's thick, scaly body was over eighty feet long and ten feet around. Its red piercing eyes and sharp fangs caused the bravest people to tremble, and its roar thundered through the valley. The people living in the nearby villages were in constant fear of the awful monster.

The serpent ate sheep grazing on the mountainsides and the oxen that pulled the carts of the villagers. It ate travelers passing through the valley, officials trying to reason with it, and brave fighters who attacked it. Then the serpent made a terrible demand. It would eat less if, once a year, villagers brought a young girl to its cave. So, on the first day of the eighth month of every year, the villagers delivered a young girl to the entrance of the serpent's cave. With a roar, the serpent would emerge from the cave and with one gulp would swallow the girl. This terrible event occurred every year for nine years.

LOOK IT UP

For more on dragon slaying myths: Dragon of Wantley, Dragon as a Symbol, Saint George and the dragon, Heracles and the Hydra, Fu Hsi Dragon, Siegfried and the Dragon Fafnir

In the tenth year, the villagers sadly began to look for another young girl to feed to the serpent. One village family, with six daughters and no sons, was chosen to give up a daughter. Li Tan and his wife had until the next morning to decide which daughter it would be.

This couple loved all their daughters equally and did not want to give up any of them. Then the youngest daughter, Li Chi, came to Li Tan. "Father," she said, "I will go. We are poor, and you have many mouths to feed. One of us must go. Why shouldn't it be me?" Li Tan and his wife refused to let Li Chi go, for they loved her too much.

REREAD

Inference

What do you learn about Li Chi from this paragraph?

121

But Li Chi was determined. When night fell, she went to the **mayor's** house and spoke to the mayor and the other officials. She **volunteered** herself as the one to go to the serpent. What she wanted, though, was to fight the serpent. After all, she was strong. She worked hard doing farm chores. Why should she just hand herself over to be swallowed up?

The mayor and the officials laughed. How could a mere girl kill the serpent when strong men had failed? Since they felt sorry for her, they did give her an old sword and a dog to take with her. They were sure they would never see them, or her, again.

On the following morning at daybreak, Li Chi and the dog set off for the serpent's cave. The villagers followed behind and stood watching from a distance. At the cave's entrance Li Chi stopped and waited. Soon the serpent's roar shook the air. From inside the cave came the hot steam of serpent breath. Then the terrible monster appeared, its red eyes glowing like embers. It flicked its tongue back and forth, eager to feast on Li Chi.

Li Chi was not afraid and neither was the dog. The dog leaped at the serpent and bit down fiercely on its ear. The serpent turned quickly, **flinging** the dog off. In that moment Li Chi ran forward and thrust the sword into the serpent's side. But the scales were too thick, and the sword did not pierce the serpent's skin. Roaring, the serpent turned back toward Li Chi. Again the dog attacked, this time biting hard into the serpent's tail. The serpent opened its mouth, howling in pain. Again Li Chi ran forward. This time, she thrust the sword into the roof of the serpent's mouth. With a mighty roar, the serpent toppled over, dead.

The villagers cheered. Li Chi had saved her village. The mayor **praised** her and sent a report to the Emperor. The Emperor was so impressed that he had Li Chi sent to the capital city so he could meet her. In time, she married a prince. Her father was made magistrate of a large **province**, and her family was given riches. Best of all, from that day to this the land has been free of serpents.

STOP AND THINK

1. How did Li Chi use quick thinking to help her in her fight?

2. How can great courage make up for small size?

The Troll's CAPE

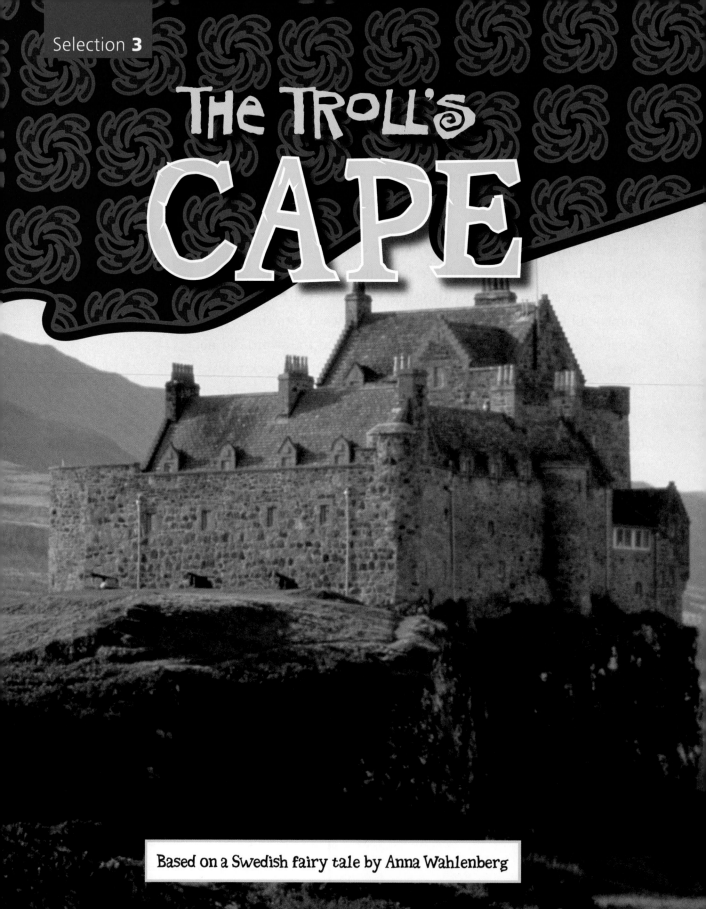

Based on a Swedish fairy tale by Anna Wahlenberg

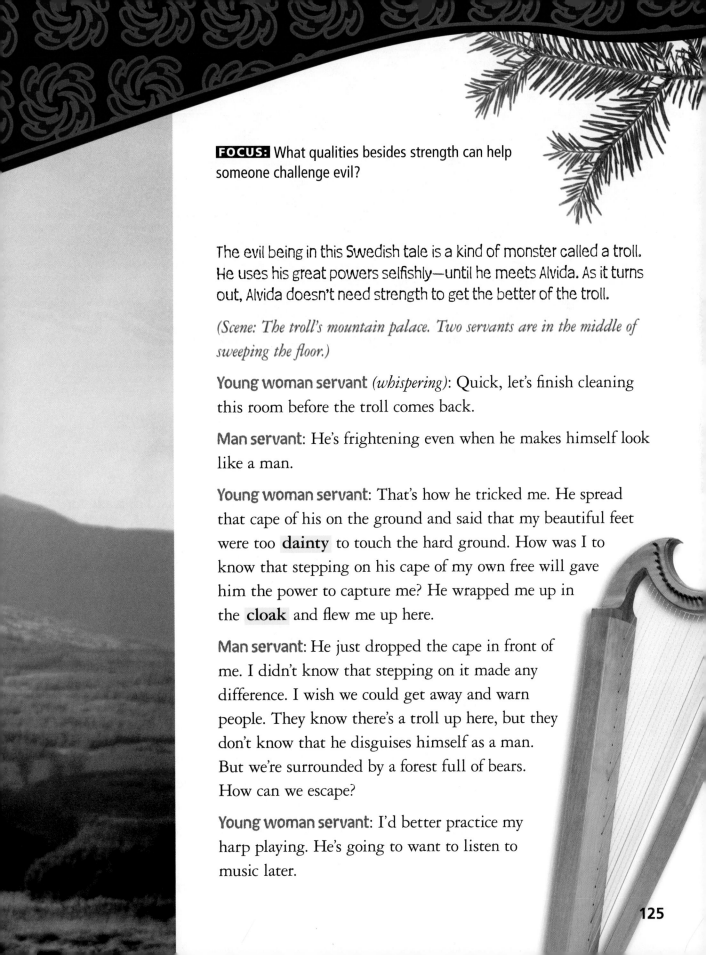

The evil being in this Swedish tale is a kind of monster called a troll. He uses his great powers selfishly—until he meets Alvida. As it turns out, Alvida doesn't need strength to get the better of the troll.

(Scene: The troll's mountain palace. Two servants are in the middle of sweeping the floor.)

Young woman servant *(whispering)*: Quick, let's finish cleaning this room before the troll comes back.

Man servant: He's frightening even when he makes himself look like a man.

Young woman servant: That's how he tricked me. He spread that cape of his on the ground and said that my beautiful feet were too **dainty** to touch the hard ground. How was I to know that stepping on his cape of my own free will gave him the power to capture me? He wrapped me up in the **cloak** and flew me up here.

Man servant: He just dropped the cape in front of me. I didn't know that stepping on it made any difference. I wish we could get away and warn people. They know there's a troll up here, but they don't know that he disguises himself as a man. But we're surrounded by a forest full of bears. How can we escape?

Young woman servant: I'd better practice my harp playing. He's going to want to listen to music later.

125

(*The scene shifts to the village. The troll, who looks just like a handsome man, is walking down a path. He's wearing a black velvet cape.*)

Troll (*to himself*): I'm bored with all my servants. I'm ready for some new ones.

(*A young woman walks by. She is Alvida, the* blacksmith's *daughter. She is humming to herself as she picks berries.*)

Troll (*to himself*): I'll take that one. (*To Alvida*): Good morning, ma'am. What a lovely day.

Alvida: Yes, isn't it? The strawberries are nice and ripe, too.

Troll (*spreading his cape on the ground*): A beautiful lady such as you shouldn't have your dainty feet touch the ground.

Alvida (*laughing*): Beautiful? Not me! And you should take better care of that fine cape. Look how it's getting covered with earth and pine needles. (*She picks it up, shakes it out, and hands it to the troll.*) Thank you for your politeness, though. (*She leaves.*)

Troll: Rats! Now I'll have to try again tomorrow.

*(The next day. The troll, disguised as a man, is near a bush. He has his cape, of course. A ram is **grazing** nearby. Alvida is just approaching.)*

Troll *(to himself)*: I'll just throw some pebbles at the ram as she passes him. When he charges her, I'll throw down the cape…and she'll run right onto it. *(He bends down, picks up some pebbles, and throws them.)* A perfect hit! He's after her…and here she comes…*(He throws his cape down, but she swerves toward the bush, while the ram runs for the cape.)* Oh, no! The ram's coming at me, and she isn't. Oh, no! Get off my cape, ram! *(He pulls at the cape. The ram runs off.)*

Alvida: Are you all right, sir? Did that ram's horns rip your fine cape?

Troll *(**clenching** his teeth)*: Yes, they did.

Alvida: I feel responsible, since it was chasing me. Here, let me take this thorn and stitch up the rip. I've used thorns as needles before, and a few strands of my hair will make the perfect thread. I'll punch a hole in this thorn with another one…there. That makes the needle's eye. Now I can thread my hair through the eye, and I'll just sew it up. *(She sews.)* There! You can't even see the stitching. Oh, you dropped part of it.

Troll: And you stepped on it, finally. *(Troll now looks like a troll. He wraps her in the cape.)*

Alvida *(from inside the cape)*: HELP! Get me out of here!

Troll: How did this branch get tangled in my cape? What? The stitching is caught on the bush! Stop squirming, girl! I have to—

Alvida: Mmph! *(She struggles free and runs as fast as she can.)*

Troll: Curses! This cape is still caught on the bush. It's as if the thread is holding onto the branch. I'll never catch that girl now.

(Later, in the troll's palace. Servants are listening to a roaring sound nearby.)

Young woman servant: Quick! Get out of his way. He's back and he's **furious** .

Man servant: Oh, he's roaring. That has to be bad.

Older woman servant *(from under a big table)*: There's room for one of you under here. *(The young woman crawls under the table to hide, while the man ducks behind a tall, wide chair.)*

Troll *(stamping through the room, carrying his cape)*: Rrrrr! That awful girl! *(He stamps upstairs. After a moment, both women, the man, and several other servants come out from their hiding places.)*

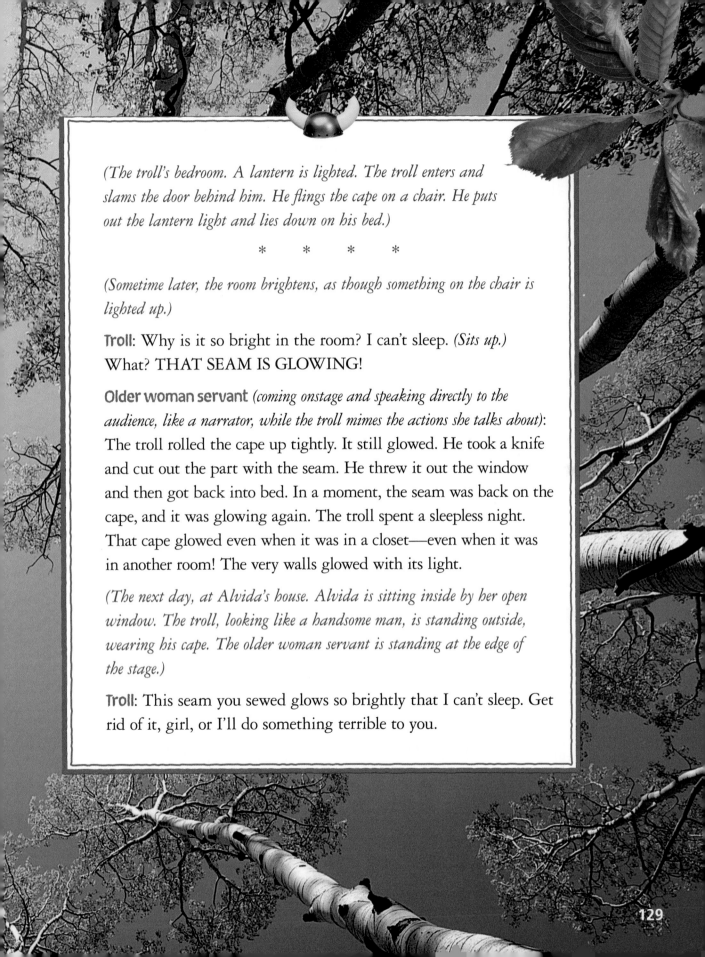

(The troll's bedroom. A lantern is lighted. The troll enters and slams the door behind him. He flings the cape on a chair. He puts out the lantern light and lies down on his bed.)

*   *   *   *

(Sometime later, the room brightens, as though something on the chair is lighted up.)

Troll: Why is it so bright in the room? I can't sleep. *(Sits up.)* What? THAT SEAM IS GLOWING!

Older woman servant *(coming onstage and speaking directly to the audience, like a narrator, while the troll mimes the actions she talks about)*: The troll rolled the cape up tightly. It still glowed. He took a knife and cut out the part with the seam. He threw it out the window and then got back into bed. In a moment, the seam was back on the cape, and it was glowing again. The troll spent a sleepless night. That cape glowed even when it was in a closet—even when it was in another room! The very walls glowed with its light.

(The next day, at Alvida's house. Alvida is sitting inside by her open window. The troll, looking like a handsome man, is standing outside, wearing his cape. The older woman servant is standing at the edge of the stage.)

Troll: This seam you sewed glows so brightly that I can't sleep. Get rid of it, girl, or I'll do something terrible to you.

Alvida: I know what you are now, Troll. And you know that a troll can't come into a human's house unless it's invited. I'm not going anywhere near your cape.

Troll *(stamping his foot)*: All right, all right. What do you want—gold? jewels?

Alvida *(after thinking for a moment)*: Here's what I want. I know you have captured a lot of other people. Set everyone in your palace free. Bring them here so I can see them. Then I'll help you.

Older woman servant *(speaking to the audience)*: What could the troll do? He had to let everyone go.

(Later, in the forest. The troll, looking like a troll, is leading all his servants out.)

Troll: This way, everyone. I'll take you back through the forest myself. Bears won't come near you if I'm here.

Young woman servant: He's letting us out? What made him decide to do that?

Man servant: Maybe someone strong made him do it.

Older woman servant: There's the edge of the forest. Run now, everyone!

Troll: Well, there go all my servants. Grrr! I'll just wait until nightfall and then go find Alvida. If I go while it's daylight, everybody for miles around will attack me. At night, they'll all be hiding in their houses.

(Night falls. The stage darkens until it is completely dark.)

Troll: What's this? That awful seam isn't glowing. Maybe it stopped because I let everyone go. Good thing trolls can see in the dark. I guess I don't have to go visit that **tiresome** girl. *(He can be heard walking away.)* It'll be good to get some sleep again. On the other hand, I won't be able to have servants ever again. Unless...I guess I can hire some.

(A week later. Alvida is sitting in front of her home, reading a newspaper. Several of the troll's former servants are sitting with her. The older woman servant is standing at the front of the stage, facing the audience.)

Alvida: Oh, look, here's an ad for servants up at the troll's palace. "Fair wages paid, one day off a week."

Young woman servant: I think I'll keep working down here.

Older woman servant *(addressing the audience directly)*: So the troll had servants again. This time, he paid them a **salary** and treated them fairly, and they did good work. When he needed to scare someone, he went outside the palace gates and roared at the bears. They roared back, and everyone had a fine time. Nobody bothered the villagers again.

■■■ STOP AND THINK

1. Would you say that Alvida was brave? Explain.

2. How can one person's behavior change the behavior of another person?

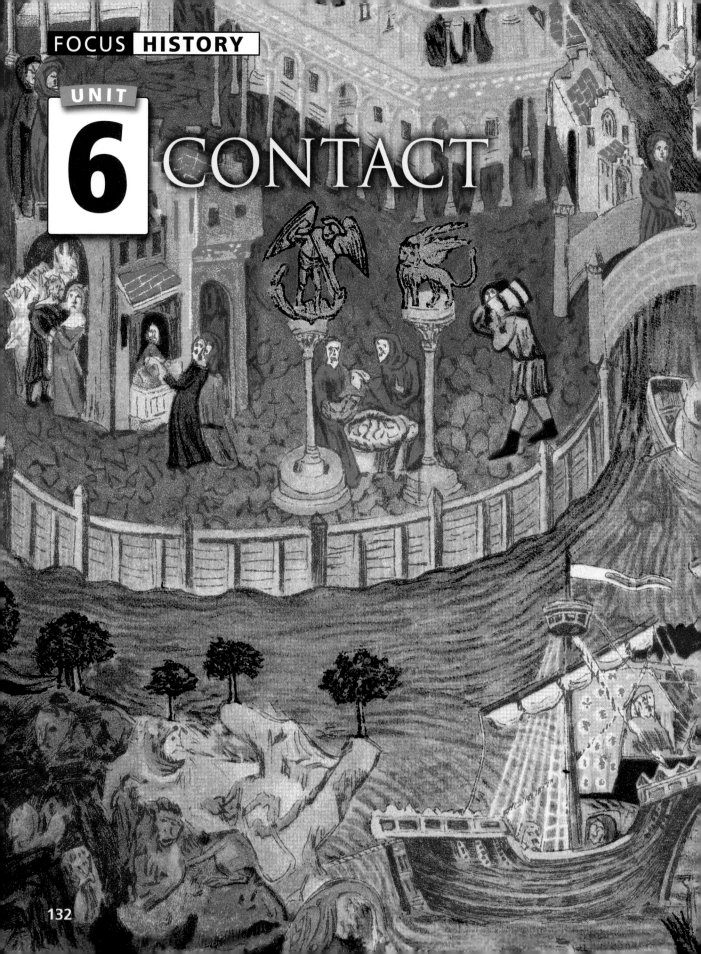

UNIT 6 CONTACT

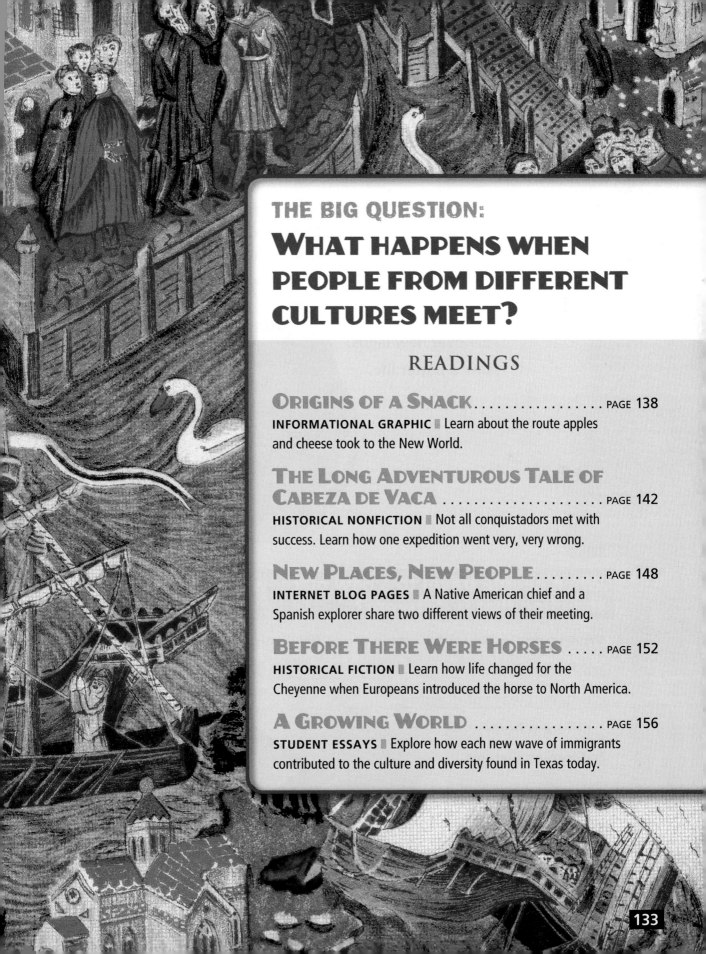

LOOK AT HOW PEOPLE MAKE CONTACT

Why do people travel far to new places?

People travel far to new places to...

- ☐ find gold.
- ☐ trade goods.
- ☐ discover new lands.
- ☐ find a better life.

When people travel to a new place, what might they find that is different?

When people travel to a new place they might find...

- ☐ different food.
- ☐ different ways of dressing.
- ☐ different homes.
- ☐ different customs.

Before there were horses in North America, how did people get around?

Before there were horses in North America...

☐ people used canoes.

☐ people walked.

☐ people used dogs to pull sleds.

☐ people couldn't travel very far.

What do we mean when we say a community is diverse?

When we say a community is diverse, we mean that...

☐ people there are doing different jobs.

☐ people there like to have fun.

☐ people there have many different ways of life.

☐ people there are from different backgrounds and cultures.

When people move to a new place, what do they bring with them?

When people move to a new place, they bring...

☐ their customs.

☐ their language.

☐ their traditional food.

☐ their skills and ideas.

History Words

barge

comrades

conquest

exhausted

expedition

fleet

harsh

ill

misfortune

ration

barge

A **barge** is a wide boat with a flat bottom.

“The barge carried goods up and down the river.”

comrades

Comrades are people who do the same job or belong to the same group.

“John and Jake were comrades who worked on the same ship.”

fleet

A **fleet** is a group of boats commanded by one person.

“There were 20 ships in the fleet, all under the command of Captain West.”

harsh

Harsh means unpleasant or very rough.

“The harsh wind made the ship toss and turn in the high waves.”

conquest

Conquest is the act of conquering, or taking over, a nation or people.

❝ In the conquest of Mexico, the Aztecs were defeated and their land was claimed by Spain. ❞

exhausted

Exhausted means very tired and out of energy.

❝ The players were so exhausted after the game they could hardly keep their eyes open. ❞

expedition

An **expedition** is a journey with a specific goal or objective.

❝ The explorers went on an expedition to discover new lands. ❞

ill

Ill means sick or unhealthy.

❝ Kim didn't like being ill, so when she started coughing she took medicine right away. ❞

misfortune

Misfortune is bad luck.

❝ It was Juan's misfortune that he arrived just seconds after the bus had left the station. ❞

ration

A **ration** is a specific amount of food given to members of a group.

❝ The hiker put her ration for the day in her backpack, where she could find it when she became hungry. ❞

Origins of a Snack

How Many Worlds Had to Meet?

Where do foods come from? Throughout history, different worlds have made contact with each other. When they met, they shared knowledge and goods—and foods. What about a snack of cheddar cheese and apples? How many worlds had to meet before this became a popular snack?

CHEESE

6000 B.C.E.

Tribes in the Middle East discover how to make a cheese that resembles today's yogurt.

450 B.C.E.

The Roman **Empire** conquers parts of the Middle East. Knowledge of cheese-making begins to spread through the empire.

40 C.E.

The Roman Empire conquers parts of Britain. People in Britain learn how to make cheese.

APPLES

8000 B.C.E.

Trade and military **expeditions** spread wild apples from the area around Kazakhstan to the Mediterranean region.

6500 B.C.E.

Greeks begin to plant apple orchards. Knowledge of orchard planting spreads across Europe.

44 B.C.E.

Farmers of the Roman Empire begin **cultivating** apples. Apples travel to Britain with the Romans.

138

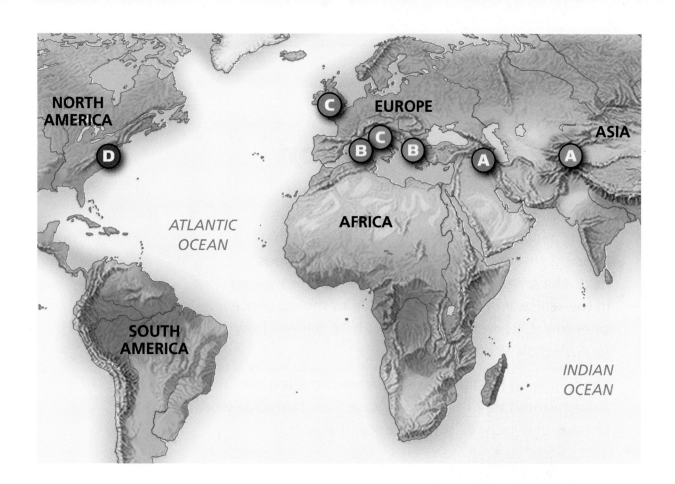

1620 C.E.

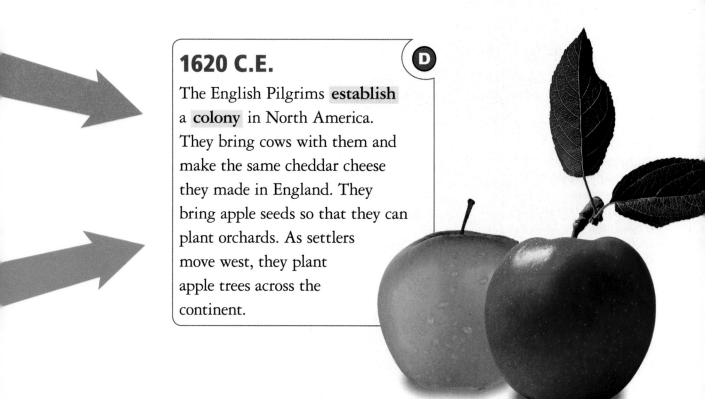

The English Pilgrims **establish** a **colony** in North America. They bring cows with them and make the same cheddar cheese they made in England. They bring apple seeds so that they can plant orchards. As settlers move west, they plant apple trees across the continent.

Comprehension

✓ **TARGET SKILL** **Sequence of Events** Most selections tell about events that happen. These events happen in an order, beginning with what happens first and continuing with what happens next. The order ends when there are no more events in the selection. This order is known as the sequence of events. Clue words and phrases help tell you how to put events in order.

The following paragraph, taken from the selection "The Long Adventurous tale of Cabeza de Vaca," contains clue words and phrases that help tell the sequence of events.

> Right from the start, Narváez made terrible decisions. After the fleet landed, he left the ships behind. He led 300 of his men on foot to find gold. They had only a few rations. Soon their food ran out. After two weeks, Narváez and his men arrived in a small American Indian village. They were exhausted.

The clue phrase *Right from the start* tells that Narváez made terrible decisions at the very beginning. The rest of the paragraph describes what happened, and the order of events.

The clue words *after* and *soon* help tell the sequence of events. They are signal words that tell the reader that the author is giving a sense of time order.

First: The fleet landed.

Second: Narváez left the ships behind.

Third: He led his men on foot to find gold.

Fourth: Their food ran out.

Fifth: They arrived exhausted in a small American Indian village.

The first box tells about the first event that happens in the sequence of events. The subsequent boxes continue the sequence and tell about each event that follows. The fifth box tells about the last thing that happens.

✔ **TARGET STRATEGY** **Summary**

As you read, stop from time to time to think about the order of events. This information can help you summarize the selection. When you summarize, you tell about the most important events in the order they occurred.

The Long Adventurous Tale of CABEZA de VACA

FOCUS: How does Cabeza de Vaca change during his adventure?

This is the story of Alvar Núñez Cabeza de Vaca. It should have been just another story of Spanish **conquest**. But when Cabeza de Vaca landed in North America, nothing went as expected.

In 1528, a Spanish expedition sailed to present-day Florida. The men were supposed to look for gold and silver. They were supposed to claim the land and its people for Spain. But things went very wrong. By the time the trip was over, only four men would still be alive. One of those men was Alvar Núñez Cabeza de Vaca.

Dreams of Gold

Pánfilo de Narváez, the commander of the Florida expedition, was a **conquistador**. Right from the start, Narváez made terrible decisions. After the fleet landed, he left the ships behind. He led 300 of his men on foot to find gold. They had only a few rations. Soon their food ran out. After two weeks, Narváez and his men arrived in a small American Indian village. They were exhausted.

The Indians fed the men. Soon the men were feeling stronger and they set out again.

Left Behind

Throughout the summer, the Spaniards looked for gold. Finally, they gave up and headed back to the shore. They expected their ships to be waiting for them. Sadly, the fleet had sailed away.

Cabeza de Vaca believed they needed ships to survive. He organized the men. By late September, they had built five **barges**.

conquistador One of the Spanish conquerers of the Americas.

Shipwrecked!

The barges set out across the Gulf of Mexico. Storms rocked the flimsy ships. The men were so sick and weak they couldn't fight the waves. Cabeza de Vaca commanded one of the barges. After a night of especially bad weather, three of the barges were gone. Narváez and more than 200 men were lost at sea. A huge wave later washed over the last two barges. Cabeza de Vaca and 87 men were washed onto an island.

The Isle of Misfortune

The island was home to the Karankawa Indians. The Karankawas shared what little bounty they had. Then they carried Cabeza de Vaca and his men away from the cold, windy shore. The Spaniards spent the harsh winter in the Karankawas' villages. Many Indians and Spaniards starved to death or died of illness. Only fifteen Spaniards survived the winter. Cabeza de Vaca named the island "The Isle of **Misfortune**."

Conquistadors had to fight through dense cypress forests in Florida.

An Unusual Journey

For the next eight years, Cabeza de Vaca lived among American Indians. Sometimes he was a slave. Sometimes he was a healer. Sometimes he was a trader. Along the way, he walked thousands of miles.

Cabeza de Vaca lives among the Karankawa Indians. He stays with them through winters and summers. He lives as they live. He no longer wears Spanish clothes. He no longer has food served to him. Now he wears very little, and he eats only the food that he hunts himself.

The Karankawas make Cabeza de Vaca a medicine man. They teach him how to heal. He uses hot rocks and sharpened seashells to make people well. Cabeza de Vaca performs surgery. The Indians give him food in exchange for his healing skills.

Cabeza de Vaca survives a terrible illness. The Karankawas think healers should not get sick, so they take away his healing tools. Now he is treated as a slave. He must carry supplies for the tribe and fetch their firewood.

In 1530, Cabeza de Vaca escapes the Karankawas. For two years he travels north and west. He moves farther into present-day Texas. He lives and trades with other American Indians. He learns to admire their way of life.

After five years, Cabeza de Vaca discovers three other survivors from his expedition. The four men decide to look for a Spanish settlement in Mexico. They follow a route that leads them 2,000 miles out of their way.

In 1536, Cabeza de Vaca and his **comrades** learn that other Spaniards have arrived in the New World. The new conquistadors have been sent to take American Indians as slaves. Cabeza de Vaca was once a conquistador. Now he feels he must defend the American Indians. He fears the slave hunters will kill him, but he speaks to them anyway. He convinces them not to hurt anybody.

In June 1536, Cabeza de Vaca and his comrades finally make it to Mexico City. When he gets back home to Spain in 1538, he writes the remarkable story of his ten-year journey.

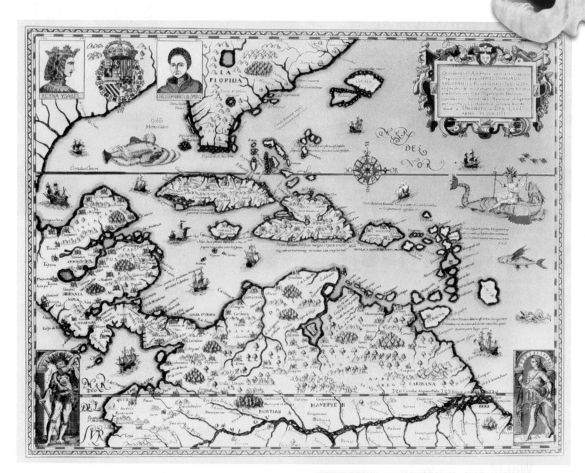

A map from the time of Cabeza de Vaca

■ ■ ■ **STOP AND THINK**

1. What were some of the things Cabeza de Vaca had to overcome?

2. Do you think you could have survived with Cabeza de Vaca? Explain.

145

Your Turn
Use Your Words:

accuse	generation
appoint	immigrate
bear	passage
bounty	patient
colony	persecute
cultivate	provision
diverse	resist
empire	ritual
establish	separate
fertile	wealthy

- Read the words on the list.
- Read the dialogue. Find the words.

The Spanish empire established a colony on the island. A governor was appointed to rule.

MORE ACTIVITIES

1. Take a Survey
Graphic Organizer

Plans are underway to start a colony on the Moon. Would you go? Ask ten classmates whether or not they would be willing to help establish a colony on the Moon. Tally their answers. Share your findings with your class.

**Would you move to
a new colony on the Moon?**

Yes	No

2. Make an Ad
Listening and Speaking

Draw an ad convincing people to come to the colony discussed in the picture above. Share your ad with your partner. Talk about ways you can make your ad more convincing.

3. Make a List
Vocabulary

Think of all the reasons people have for moving from one place to another. Make a list. Share your list with your class.

4. Provisions and Tools

Listening and Speaking

What would you bring to a new colony? Think of three important items for each of these categories: clothing, tools, food. Share your list with your class. Talk about why these items are important.

5. You Are the Author

Writing

Imagine you have just arrived at a faraway land. Write an e-mail to a friend back home telling about all the new things you see and hear.

6. Museum Exhibit

Listening and Speaking

Choose one of the museum exhibits from the picture. What would you tell about it? Write two or three sentences telling about the exhibit. Share your sentences with your partner.

NEW PLACES, NEW PEOPLE

FOCUS: What led to this meeting between Spaniards and the Chumash?

On October 10, 1542, three Spanish ships sailed into what is now the Santa Barbara Channel of California. The leader of the expedition was Juan Rodríguez Cabrillo. Cabrillo met the first Californians on record, the Chumash Indians.

Juan Rodríguez Cabrillo

"Give me a good ship and some uncharted territory, and I'll be a happy man."

I am male.

I am in my 40s.

I live in a cabin on the **flagship** *San Salvador*.

 Send Message

 Add to Friends

 Instant Message

About Me

I was born in Portugal, but I consider myself Spanish. I served in the army of Hernán Cortés. I took part in the conquest of Mexico and Guatemala, helping to defeat the Aztecs. In 1532, I went to Spain, where I met and married Beatriz Sánchez de Ortega. We moved to Guatemala and had two sons. By the mid-1530s I had an import-export business and a ship-building company.

My reputation for building ships got me an **appointment** to help expand Spain's empire. This is the first European expedition to the west coast of the New World. My goal is to find a **passage** that connects the North Pacific and the North Atlantic Oceans. We have enough **provisions** for two years.

------

flagship Ship that carries the commander of a fleet.

Latest Blog Entry

October 10, 1542 — Tuesday

This morning, we sailed into a beautiful channel. We could see a large valley. Along the shore are some **pueblos** of good size. After we anchored, a fleet of large and well-built canoes came swiftly toward the ship. Each of the canoes held twelve or thirteen Indians. I invited them to come aboard. The Indian men are tall and muscular, and wear little clothing. They were friendly to us. They brought us gifts of fish to eat. I gave them gifts in return. They seemed very pleased.

My comrades and I went ashore. As soon as we landed, I claimed the land for Spain. The natives watched in wonder as I completed the ceremony of possession. I chose to name the village *Pueblo de Las Canoas* because of the Indians' fine canoes. I do not expect to learn much from the natives. They are friendly, but they cannot understand the ways of our world. Nor can I understand theirs. They have a large mud-covered hut. Smoke comes from a large hole on the top. Men and women climb in and out of the hole. I wonder what the purpose of the curious hut is.

---

pueblo American Indian village of the southwestern United States.

149

NEW PLACES, NEW PEOPLE

Wansak

"Everything changes. It is only natural."

I am male.

I am in my 20s.

I live in Shisholop, in an *'ap*, or hut.

 Send Message

 Add to Friends

Instant Message

About Me

I was born in the village of Shisholop. My people are called the Chumash. We are so named because we make shell beads that we use for money. The word *michumash* means "those who make shell-bead money."

My grandmother was the *wot,* or chief, of Shisholop until she died. Then my father became *wot.* Someday, I will take over the job. I have not married yet, because I am too busy. I build the *tomols,* or canoes, that we use for fishing and traveling. Without them, we would not be able to trade seeds, acorns, animal skins, hunting tools, and baskets with other villages.

When I have free time, I like to play *tikauwich*, a game with sticks and a puck. I often make goals by hitting the puck all the way from my side of the field.

Latest Blog Entry

An autumn day, 1542

[Subscribe to this Blog]
Comments

Today, a strange event took place. I was working on a new *tomol*, scraping planks by the shore. I looked up and saw a huge boat coming toward the village. All the men of my village got in our *tomols* and paddled quickly out to the big boat. Nobody had ever seen such a boat. The sides curved up to the sky. Skins to catch the wind soared overhead. As we got closer, we could see men on board. They had pale skin and hair on their faces. They wore clothes from head to foot. I thought they must feel quite hot. The leader invited us on board and gave us gifts of beads. We gave them fish.

Soon, they came to shore. The leader made a strange **ritual**. He spoke some words while holding a sharp, shiny stick. He then cut a tree and moved some rocks. Finally, he poured water from the sea onto the land. The leader seemed fascinated by our *'apa'yik,* or sweathouse. I wonder whether he wanted to climb inside and cleanse himself.

> **REREAD**
>
> **Sequence of Events**
>
> What happened after the leader spoke some words and before he poured water onto the land?

STOP AND THINK

1. Which two cultures met on October 10, 1542?

2. Would you rather have been part of Cabrillo's expedition or a member of Wansak's village? Why?

BEFORE THERE WERE HORSES

Three Sioux on horseback

FOCUS: How did horses change life for the Cheyenne?

NORTH DAKOTA, 1794

Minninnewah was lying on a flat rock beside a stream. He had just bathed, and was cool and refreshed. Behind him, the horses shuffled impatiently. They were tired and dirty.

"You'll get your turn," he said. "I'm relaxing now. I can't make you happy until I'm happy, can I?"

"Minninnewah! Why are you not finished washing the horses?" Minninnewah's grandmother was trudging through the tall grass.

Minninnewah jumped to his feet. "I'm almost done, Grandmother," he said.

Grandmother reached the bank of the gurgling stream. Her old face was lined and wrinkled. She lowered herself onto the rock and patted the place beside her. Minninnewah sat down. Grandmother gazed across the stream to the **fertile** plains beyond. Minninnewah followed her gaze. "The hunt was good today, boy?" she asked.

Minninnewah was surprised at the question. He was ready to

be scolded for not washing the horses. He was used to being scolded. Just yesterday he had been scolded for breaking a **travois**. A travois must be loaded carefully. But Minninnewah didn't have the **patience** to place things just so. He had loaded too much on one side, and one of the poles snapped in half.

"It was a very good day for hunting, Grandmother," he said. "We took the horses out early, before the day became too hot. We rode fast to reach the buffalo, and as soon as they heard the horses, they began to run." Minninnewah smiled at the memory. "The horses never lost their nerve or **resisted**. Our aim was true. We will have plenty to eat and there will be many new skins to **tan**. It was a very good day."

"It is clear you love the hunt," said Grandmother. "But you do not love the horses that allow you to hunt."

"But I do!" Minninnewah cried, upset at the **accusation**.

"Look at them. There they stand, hot and tired. Here you sit, cool and clean." Before he could say anything, she went on. "I will tell you, Little Whirlwind, why you should love the horses better than you do."

Grandmother settled herself more comfortably on the rock.

An American Indian on a horse pulling a travois

travois Animal-drawn vehicle made of two trailing poles and a platform, used by Plains Indians to transport loads.
tan To turn hide into leather.

Hide painting from the Plains Indian Museum

"There was a time, many years ago, when our people did not have horses. Then, several **generations** ago, the white men came. The pale-faced men seemed to be very tall. And they had four legs, instead of two."

Minninnewah laughed. "Four legs? They were only men, weren't they? Why did they have four legs like animals?"

"They only seemed to have four legs," Grandmother explained. "No one had ever seen a man on a horse. Our people did not understand that they were two **separate** creatures. Soon, though, they saw that the horse was a special animal that seemed to belong in our land.

"Herds of wild horses began to roam the plains. The Cheyenne were natural riders. We traded for some horses, but also captured and tamed the powerful animals.

"Before we had horses, our lives were very different. We had dogs to pull the travois, but they were not able to pull much weight. We hunted the buffalo, even back then. But we did so on foot, and it was dangerous to get too close. In those days, we lived mostly in one place, growing corn and other foods. It was difficult to grow enough for the whole tribe, and the winters were hard.

"Horses changed all that. Our hunters could get much closer to the buffalo. We had more food. No longer did we starve during the long winters. We could travel great distances because horses could **bear** heavy loads.

"Now we go where the buffalo are. We live in open spaces so the horses can roam." Grandmother paused and looked back at the horses. "Our people feel a great connection to horses. When we tamed them, we made a promise to care for them as well." She looked at Minninnewah.

He got up and led the horses into the stream. "Grandmother," he said, "I don't believe I have ever been scolded so well." He stroked the side of a horse. "And I believe it is the last time it will be needed."

■■■ STOP AND THINK

1. What lesson did Minninnewah learn from his grandmother?

2. Why do you think she told a story rather than scold him?

Four American Indians near their homes

💻 LOOK IT UP

For more on the history of horses and humans: domestication of horses, Plains Indians and horses, horse culture

FOCUS: Can different worlds meet in one state?

The Assignment
A teacher gave her class this assignment.

It has been many years since European colonists met other worlds for the first time. We can find the evidence of these meetings all around us. It is in the food we eat. It is in the music we listen and dance to. It is in the languages we speak. Mostly, it is in the faces of the people who make up our world.

Do some research about Texas. Write a report. It should tell about the worlds that met to make our state what it is today.

The Reports
Here are some of the reports the students wrote.

Spanish and Indian Texas
by Vicky Yan

In the 1600s, the Spanish Empire settled the area that is now Texas. The Spanish didn't establish big cities in Texas. They thought of Texas as a border province. It was meant to protect their empire from attacks.

Most Spanish settlers in Texas lived far apart from one another, on ranches. There, they raised livestock such as cattle, sheep, and horses.

Ranching is important in Texas to this day. Spanish livestock also caused a change that the Empire couldn't have predicted. Before the Spanish came, the Indians of the Americas had never seen horses. Having seen the Spaniards ride, the American Indians desperately wanted the animals. In a very short time, some groups of American Indians became fine riders. The use of horses spread across the Great Plains. Thus, the contact with Spanish settlers changed the Plains Indians' way of life.

Mexican Texas
by Julie Cartwright

The men and women of Spanish Texas called themselves *Tejanos* and *Tejanas.* These names simply meant "Texans" in Spanish. In 1821, Mexico, including Texas, gained its freedom from Spain. *Tejanos* and *Tejanas* continued to live mostly on ranches. **Wealthy** landowners hired *vaqueros,* or "cowmen," to tend the cattle.

Vaqueros worked mostly from horseback. They used a looped rope called a *lazo* to capture cattle. They wore leather pants called *chaps.* These protected their legs from thorns and brush.

Once a year, *Tejano* ranchers would have a *rodeo,* or cattle roundup. The herd would be inspected. Everyone in the ranch community gathered together for the roundup. This gave *vaqueros* a ready audience to watch them show off their riding skills. The rodeo of today comes from those roundups.

In the 1820s, another group of settlers **immigrated** to Texas. These settlers came from the United States. They called themselves Texians. Some Texians cultivated cotton. Others took up cattle ranching. Texian ranch hands adopted the *vaqueros'* skills and equipment. They used *vaqueros'* outfits and even their vocabulary. That's how English-speaking cowboys came to rope cattle with a lasso, wear protective leather chaps, and take part in rodeos.

Even today, the *Tejano* past is still a strong part of Texan culture. You can hear it in the guitar music. You can taste it in the chili. Perhaps the strongest proof can be seen at any rodeo. When you see a rodeo performer, you're watching someone whose skills come from the *vaqueros* of Mexican Texas.

African Americans in Texas
by Pham Kiet

The history of African Americans in Texas is unique. When settlers from the southern U.S. states came into Texas in the 1820s, they brought enslaved workers with them.

Texas joined the Confederacy in the Civil War. The war ended in April 1865. However, African Americans in Texas didn't hear the news until June 19th 1865. On that date, African Americans realized that slavery had ended in the newly reunited United States. "Juneteenth" became a celebration in African American communities all over Texas. Today, the date is marked with dances, picnics, dramatic readings, parades, and music festivals.

> **REREAD**
>
> **Sequence of Events**
>
> How does the author show the order of events in this section?

Vietnamese Texans
by Jesse Brown

The large cities in Texas are very **diverse**. Some Texans have local roots going back over 100 years. Others arrived more recently. Some came to Texas to escape **persecution** in their old countries. Others came to look for better opportunities. For example, the city of Houston has a large Vietnamese community. Many came from Southeast Asia after the Vietnam War ended in the 1970s. Houston now has the third-largest Vietnamese-American population in the United States. The city has Vietnamese supermarkets and restaurants. It has Vietnamese-speaking doctors and lawyers. It even has Vietnamese-speaking real estate agents.

> **STOP AND THINK**
>
> 1. Why is Texas so rich in Spanish and Mexican heritage?
> 2. Which worlds met to make your community what it is?

UNIT 7 LET'S ROCK!

CHANGES IN THE LANDSCAPE

How do we use rocks?

We use rocks to...

☐ build buildings.

☐ build bridges.

☐ build walls.

☐ make statues.

What causes an eruption?

An eruption is caused by...

☐ a tornado.

☐ an earthquake.

☐ a volcano.

☐ an avalanche.

How many kinds of rocks are there?

There are...

☐ just one kind of rock.

☐ three kinds of rocks.

☐ ten kinds of rocks.

☐ so many kinds of rocks you can't count them.

What can happen when a volcano erupts?

When a volcano erupts...

☐ lava can flow.

☐ it spews ash into the air.

☐ it can cause a mudslide.

☐ an island can form.

What causes erosion?

Erosion is caused by...

☐ wind.

☐ ice.

☐ water.

☐ gravity.

Science Words

debris

dramatic

erode

igneous

metamorphic

sedimentary

silt

situation

sludge

stable

debris

Debris is scattered, broken pieces of something.

66 After the rockslide, there was a pile of debris at the bottom of the cliff. 99

dramatic

Dramatic refers to something powerful, impressive, or exciting.

66 Erosion can create dramatic landscapes. 99

sedimentary

Sedimentary rock forms when layers of sand, gravel, or silt deposited over time are compacted.

66 Sandstone is one example of a sedimentary rock. 99

silt

Silt is very fine particles of soil.

66 The Missouri River is known as the Big Muddy because there is so much silt in the water. 99

erode

Erode means to wear away gradually.

66 Wind and water can erode rocks. 99

igneous

Igneous refers to rock formed by volcanic action.

66 The volcano created a good deal of new igneous rock. 99

metamorphic

Metamorphic refers to rock changed in form or structure by extreme pressure or heat.

66 The metamorphic rock was formed deep in the earth. 99

situation

A **situation** is the place or circumstance that something is in.

66 If your car breaks down on the highway, you could be in a difficult situation. 99

sludge

Sludge is a thick, muddy, oozing substance.

66 There was a thick sludge covering everything in the basement after the flood. 99

stable

When something is **stable**, it does not change or move easily.

66 The new building was very stable because it was anchored firmly in bedrock. 99

VOLCANOES AND THE
RING OF FIRE

The Ring of Fire

Scientists say as many as 75 percent of the earth's volcanoes are located around the edges of the Pacific Ocean. The area has so many active volcanoes, it is known as the "Ring of Fire." All this activity is a result of the earth's plates bumping, scraping, and squeezing together.

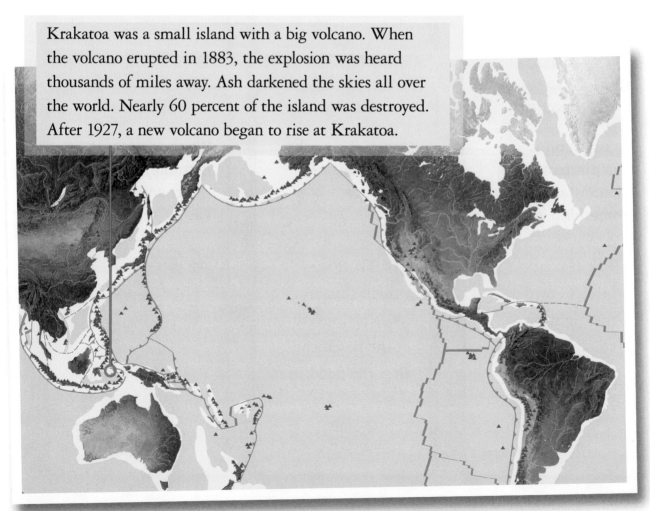

Krakatoa was a small island with a big volcano. When the volcano erupted in 1883, the explosion was heard thousands of miles away. Ash darkened the skies all over the world. Nearly 60 percent of the island was destroyed. After 1927, a new volcano began to rise at Krakatoa.

Ring of Fire Eruptions Since 1900

1991 Mt. Pinatubo, Philippines
1991 Mt. Unzen, Japan
1985 Nevada del Ruiz, Colombia
1980 Mt. St. Helens, U.S.
1951 Mt. Lamington, Papua New Guinea
1919 Kelut, Indonesia
1902 Mont Pelee, Martinique

Inside a Volcano

Comprehension

✔ **TARGET SKILL** **Compare and Contrast** When you search for ways that people, objects, events, or even ideas are similar or different, you are comparing and contrasting. Comparing is looking at how things are similar while contrasting is searching for differences between two or more things.

The following sentences are taken from the selection "How Rocks Form."

> **This explains how all rocks are related.**
>
> Rocks come in many different shapes, colors, textures, and sizes. However, all rocks can be sorted ... according to how they were formed.
>
> **Details are presented about one category of rocks.**
>
> Igneous rocks are made from hot, melted rock, either magma or lava, that cools and hardens back into rock. Igneous rocks can form when magma cools and hardens under the surface of Earth. They can also form when a volcano pushes lava into the air.
>
> **A second category of rocks is contrasted with the first.**
>
> Metamorphic rock is rock that has been changed by heat and pressure. Deep in the earth, the temperature is very high. There is enormous pressure from the weight of the rock above.

How are igneous and metamorphic rocks alike? How are they different? You can use a Venn diagram to find out. In a Venn diagram the similarities are found where the two circles overlap. The differences are placed in the outer sections of the circles.

Igneous Rock

made from hot, melted rock that cools and hardens

can be magma that cools and hardens under Earth's surface

can be lava pushed into air from volcano

Both

sorted according to how formed

Metamorphic Rock

rock changed by heat and pressure

formed deep in the earth where temperature is high and pressure enormous

✔ **TARGET STRATEGY** **Ask Questions** As you read, ask yourself questions that help you compare or contrast things in the selection. For example, are two or more items that have something in common described? Are their differences also described?

How Rocks Form

Limestone formations in the Egyptian desert

FOCUS: What conditions deep in the earth create the different kinds of rock found on the planet?

Rocks come in many different shapes, colors, textures, and sizes. However, all rocks can be sorted into three main groups according to how they were formed. There are **igneous**, **sedimentary**, and **metamorphic** rocks.

Igneous rocks are made from hot, melted rock, either magma or lava, that cools and hardens back into rock. Igneous rocks can form when magma cools and hardens under the surface of Earth. They can also form when a volcano pushes lava into the air. Igneous rock is the main kind of rock in Earth's crust. Some important kinds of igneous rock are granite, basalt, obsidian, and pumice.

Sedimentary rocks are formed from other materials. Weathering and erosion break down larger rocks into smaller rocks. Over time, smaller rocks become sand and **silt**. The small rocks, sand, silt, and other matter wash into rivers and seas. There they settle down to become a layer of sediment. Over the years, new layers of sediment are added. Each new layer pushes down on the layers below. With enough time and pressure, sediment deep below the earth's surface can become sedimentary rock. Some important sedimentary rocks are sandstone, limestone, coal, and chalk.

If you bake a piece of clay in an oven, it changes. That is a little like what happens to metamorphic rock. Metamorphic rock is rock that has been changed by heat and pressure. Deep in the earth, the temperature is very high. There is enormous pressure from the weight of the rock above. Under these conditions, shale is changed into the metamorphic rock called slate. Limestone becomes marble, and sandstone becomes very hard quartzite.

LOOK IT UP

For more on rock formation: sandstone rocks, natural crystal formation, igneous rocks, sedimentary rocks, mineral formation, gemstone formation

STOP AND THINK

1. What causes large rocks to become smaller ones?

2. Why do you think rocks that have been subjected to high heat and pressure, like marble, are especially hard?

171

Your Turn
Use your Words

architect	glacier
biologist	grit
botanist	monitor
cling	monument
data	quarry
definite	relate
device	summit
embers	urban
fascinate	whirlpool
geologist	witness

- Read the words on the list.
- Read the dialogue. Find the words.

> What does that <u>device</u> do?

> We are reporting on a very unstable situation. <u>Geologists</u> think that the <u>summit</u> of this volcano may explode. The town is a <u>whirlpool</u> of activity.

> It collects <u>data</u> that we use to <u>monitor</u> volcanic activity.

MORE ACTIVITIES

1. You Are the Newscaster
Speaking and Listening

Imagine you were reporting from the site of an erupting volcano. What would you say? Write a news report telling about the volcano. Read your report to your partner.

2. Taking Things with You
Writing

Suppose there was a natural disaster. You had to leave your home in a hurry and could take only two things. What two things would you take? Tell why.

3. Dialogue
Listening and Speaking

Have you ever seen a monument? What person or event did the monument honor? Draw a picture of the monument. Talk about it with your partner.

4. You Are the Author
Writing

What things fascinate you? Choose one of them. Write a story about it.

As an <u>urban architect</u>, that will be a great loss.

The <u>quarry</u> near the <u>glacier</u> will be covered with lava.

The drama here continues. I'm here with a <u>biologist</u>. Tell our viewers what will happen to the wildlife.

You were a <u>witness</u>, Miss. Can you <u>relate</u> what you saw?

Well, there was a <u>definite</u> boom. That's when lots of ash and <u>grit</u> began falling. Hot <u>embers</u>, too. That's when I got out of the house.

Look, ash is <u>clinging</u> to that <u>monument</u>.

That volcano does <u>fascinate</u> me, but it's scary, too.

Most of the animal life will be fine, but you should speak with a <u>botanist</u> about the plant life.

5. Make a Venn Diagram
Graphic Organizer

What things do you see near your home that are made of rock? What things do you see at school that are made of rock? What things made of rock do you find in both places?

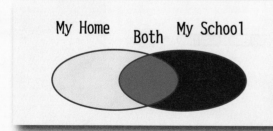

6. How Are They Different?
Vocabulary

Make two lists. Write down events you would like to witness. Then write down events that you do not want to witness.

Witness	No Way!

A VOLCANO ERUPTS

FOCUS: A volcano is a dangerous part of Earth that's always changing, but can it be more dangerous after the eruption? Explain.

NEWSFLASH

Mount Pinatubo, a volcano in the Philippines

KURT: Good evening. It is June 15, 1991, and we are interrupting regular programming to bring you this newsflash. Mount Pinatubo, a volcano in the Philippines, has erupted. This dramatic eruption is sending tons of ash into the sky. Thick blankets of ash are falling on the areas near the mountain. The ash is covering towns, roads, forests, and fields. Our reporter, Michelle Corteza, is at Clark Air Base. That's about 15 miles from the **summit** of the mountain. *(Turning to address the reporter on the monitor.)* Michelle, what can you tell us about this eruption?

MICHELLE: Kurt, this is a huge blast. The whole top of the mountain was blown away. The ash is rising 10, maybe 20, miles into the air. As you can see, it is very dark here now, even though it is the middle of the day! The sun is being blocked by the huge quantity of ash in the air. Of course, there are no real **data** at this point. However, it looks as if this may be one of the biggest volcanic eruptions in the last 100 years.

KURT: Unbelievable! With an eruption like that, there must have been hundreds, or maybe even thousands, of casualties. What's the **situation**, Michelle?

MICHELLE: Well, Kurt, the good news is that geologists here predicted this eruption. The volcano has been more and more active in the past couple of months. Geologists have been **monitoring** it very carefully. Three days ago the volcano sent a huge column of ash into the sky. After that, the scientists told the government the area had to be cleared. So, when the volcano erupted today, many of the one million people who live on or near the mountain had already been warned. Many had already left the area. We are predicting that there will be very few casualties.

Pinatubo is a stratovolcano on the island of Luzon.

Dangerous lahars form from the eruption of Mount Pinatubo.

KURT: Well, that is good news! I guess monitoring the volcano really paid off.

MICHELLE: Yes, Kurt, it certainly did. The warnings and evacuations in the past few days have undoubtedly saved thousands of lives. For example, here on Clark Air Base, 15,000 American servicepeople and their families were evacuated.

And if I could say just one more thing, Kurt: The big problem right now is that it is raining heavily. The rain is making the ash wet and heavy. This is going to cause a lot of damage as roofs give way under all the weight. Also, the water can cause the ash that has collected on the mountainside to start to flow down the mountain in a kind of mudslide that can be very dangerous. Scientists here are predicting that these mudslides will in fact cause more injuries and property damage than the eruption itself.

KURT: OK, Michelle. Well, that will be something to check on in the future. Thanks for your report. Stay safe now!

MICHELLE: Thank you, Kurt.

KURT: *(turning back to the audience)* That was Michelle Corteza reporting from Clark Air Base in the Philippines.

LOOK IT UP

For more on volcanoes: Mount Vesuvius, Pompeii, Mauna Loa Volcano, Mount Pelée, Nevado Del Ruiz

176

FIVE YEARS LATER

KURT: Today, June 15, 1996, marks five years since the eruption of Mount Pinatubo in the Philippines. It was a devastating blast—the world's biggest eruption in 75 years. A lot of progress has been made toward recovery, but many aftereffects are still being felt today. To bring you up to date, here is a special report.

SPECIAL REPORT

from Michelle Corteza

It's been five years since the eruption of Mount Pinatubo. The eruption lasted 10 hours. The aftereffects have lasted much longer. During the eruption, hot ash, **embers**, and volcanic **debris** flowed down the mountain. Deep valleys filled with as much as 600 feet of ash. These thick piles of volcanic debris are not very solid. Every time it rains, the volcanic material can become **unstable**. It can quickly turn into giant, fast-moving mudslides, or mudflows. These mudflows have a special name. They are called lahars. They are *very* dangerous.

The lahars on Mount Pinatubo usually move at about 20 miles an hour. They are about 30 feet deep and 300 feet wide. They crush, destroy, and uproot everything in their path. Think of a massive river of **sludge** as high as a three-story building and as wide as a football field coming at you faster than a galloping horse, and you have the general idea! Luckily, most of the unstable material has already come down the mountain. In a few years, the lahars will be small and uncommon.

Another piece of good news is that scientists and government officials have a very good system to warn people when a lahar starts to flow. There are **devices** to monitor rainfall and ground vibrations.

There are people who watch for mudslides in the areas that are most at risk. With all this information, government scientists can warn people almost every time there is danger. Life is slowly beginning to return to normal.

This has been Michelle Corteza in the Philippines with a special report.

STOP AND THINK

1. What happens when volcanic debris on a mountainside becomes soaked with rain?

2. How can devices that monitor rainfall and ground vibrations help people who live near an active volcano?

CITY ROCKS: An Interview with Beverley Rockhauser, Urban Geologist

FOCUS: Do you have to be a scientist in a lab to study the rocks made by our changing earth? Explain.

Many of us like looking at collections of unusual rocks in a museum. We enjoy skipping stones on the beach, scrambling over boulders on a hiking trail, or jumping from stone to stone along a creek bed. But not many of us think about rocks when we are in the city. Yet in the city, rocks are all around us. Karen Moore spoke with urban **geologist** *Dr. Beverley Rockhauser to find out more.*

Karen Moore: First of all, what is an **urban** geologist?

Dr. Rockhauser: *Urban* means *city,* and *geologists* study the earth and rocks. Urban geologists sometimes study the landforms underneath the city. They want to know if the city is built on land that is solid and safe. Others study the rocks that you find in the city. That's what I do.

KM: Where are there rocks in a city? You're not talking about pieces of rock you find in the street?

DR: No, I'm not. Of course, there are a few rocks in the street, in parks, and in people's gardens. But the most amazing rocks in the city are the ones that are hidden in plain sight. I study the rocks

The Arlington Memorial Bridge, Washington, D.C.

that are used in buildings! Beautiful and **fascinating** rocks are everywhere in the city. And there are so many different kinds. You can learn a lot from studying the rocks used to build, for example, the public library, the town hall, the courthouse, or even private homes.

KM: Do you find the same rocks in every town and city?

DR: Not at all! There's a different mix everywhere. If there is a **quarry** nearby, you may find a lot of local stone. Before railroads, it was hard to transport heavy stone over long distances. But it's amazing how much stone is shipped around the country now and even imported from overseas. For example, limestone from Indiana was used to build important buildings all across the country. You find marble from Italy all over the world.

KM: What kinds of rocks are the best for building?

Limestone from Indiana was used to build the Empire State Building.

179

The Kennedy
Center for
the Performing
Arts, Washington,
D.C.

DR: There are many kinds. There are igneous, sedimentary, and metamorphic rocks that all make excellent building materials. For example, sandstone and limestone travertine are sedimentary rocks. Granite is the most commonly used igneous rock. Marble and slate are metamorphic rocks. Builders and **architects** have a lot to choose from! They look for rocks that are strong, good-looking, easy to use, and the right price for a project.

KM: Dr. Rockhauser, you run "Urban Geology Field Trips" in Washington, D.C. What exactly does that mean?

DR: Well, the field trips are a fun mix of history, geology, architecture, and hiking! We visit some of the most famous buildings in the city. We identify the kind of stone in each building. We discuss where and when that stone was cut, or quarried. We look closely to detect the mineral composition of the stone. We also think about the geology of how the stone was formed.

KM: Can you give us some examples of famous buildings and the kinds of stone used to build them?

DR: The original Smithsonian building is made of Red Seneca rock, a sedimentary rock. It's from a quarry just 20 miles from the city. The Arlington Memorial Bridge is made of igneous granite from North Carolina. The front of the Kennedy Center for the Performing Arts is made of metamorphic Carrara marble all the way from Italy.

REREAD

Compare + Contrast

Compare and contrast the materials used to build these structures.

KM: Amazing! Finally, any advice for people who want to go on urban geology field trips in their own home towns?

DR: Keep your eyes open. Bring a magnifying glass and some rock samples, if you have them. A geologist would be useful to bring along, too, if you can borrow one! Take photographs if you can. Follow up with a trip to the library or local historical society. You can find out a lot about when and how each building was constructed and probably about the kind of stone that was used.

KM: Thanks. And thanks for the info!

The Smithsonian Institute, Washington, D.C.

STOP AND THINK

1. Before there were railroads, what kind of rocks do you think were used for buildings? Explain your answer.

2. Would you like to be an urban geologist? Why or why not?

SHAPING THE LANDSCAPE
EROSION BY WIND, WATER, ICE, GRAVITY...AND PEOPLE!

FOCUS: What forces are strong enough to change the very shape of the earth?

Wind, water, gravity, and ice can all wear away, shape, and move rock and soil. This process is called erosion.

WIND EROSION Which is stronger, rock or wind? The answer depends on how long you are willing to wait! In parts of Utah, wind won out over rock after many thousands of years. The wind, and the small bits of sand and grit the wind carried, wore away at the rock to make some amazing arches and monuments of stone.

WATER EROSION Water can carve the steep sides of canyons. Water is one of the most powerful forces that shape the landscape. Streams and rivers wear away at rock. They carry silt, soil, pebbles, and small rocks downstream. Pounding ocean waves change the shape of the shore. Ice, especially the huge ice mountains called glaciers, can also cause erosion. As glaciers creep slowly along, they carve, shape, and scrape the land underneath them.

REREAD

Compare **+** Contrast

Compare and contrast the ways in which wind and water cause erosion.

Water wears away the shape of this glacier.

GRAVITY AND EROSION Gravity makes rocks bump and crash down a slope. As they fall, they break other rocks and crack up themselves. This is erosion in action! Rockslides, landslides, and mudslides are also forms of erosion caused by gravity. Usually these slides happen after earthquakes or heavy rain. They are a definite danger and can cause lots of damage.

PEOPLE AND EROSION Wind, water, ice, gravity, and ... people! People can speed up the process of erosion by making changes in the land. Activities such as farming, construction, and cutting trees can make it easier for wind and water to carry away topsoil. This is bad because topsoil is very important for farming. Grass and tree roots reach down and grab the soil. When prairie grass is plowed or trees are cut down, there is nothing for the soil to **cling** to. Planting trees is a great way to fight against erosion!

> **REREAD**
>
> Compare ➕ Contrast
>
> Compare and contrast the quality of soil before and after human activities change the land.

> ◼◼◼ **STOP AND THINK**
>
> 1. Do mudslides cause erosion, or are they an effect of erosion?
>
> 2. Which force do you think is the most powerful cause of erosion? Why?

183

Smoke from an erupting underwater volcano ➤

FOCUS: Is it possible to watch Earth change in front of your eyes? Explain.

Isleifur II: Ship's Log

Tuesday, November 14, 1963. Captain Neilsson.
Location: South of Iceland, 63.4°N, 20.3°W

0500 Hours Sea mostly calm. Clear skies. Light wind from the southwest. Almost time to pull in the nets.

0655 Catch all in and stowed. Strong smell of sulfur in the air. Had the crew check the boat for any chemical spill on board, but they found nothing.

0705 We are rocking in a strange way, as if the waves are in a **whirlpool** of some kind. Can this be **related** to the smell? Is my boat in any danger?

0715 Sighted smoke on the horizon, maybe three or four miles southwest. Could it be a ship on fire?

0725 The smoke is getting thicker. What is burning? *Could this be an underwater volcanic eruption?* Heading southwest to get a better view.

0750 This is an eruption! The smoke columns are massive—rising maybe 200 feet into the air. It's thick, with ash, smoke, and steam.

0845 Have seen huge blobs of lava flying through the air, splashing into a steaming sea! Will head out to clear seas to stay safe.

1020 Finally, we are further out, away from the danger. We can see the columns of smoke. They rise maybe two or three miles into the sky!

1625 The sun is black with ash, and the sea is full of burning embers. Lightning is flashing up through the columns of smoke.

1935 We can detect something black and solid just under the surface of the water. Maybe it is a new volcanic island rising. We feel we have seen the history of Earth unfolding before our very eyes.

Epilogue

It was indeed a new volcanic island that the crew of the *Isleifur II* **witnessed** being born on November 14, 1963. Scientists named it Surtsey, after the Norse fire god *Surtr*.

The eruptions and lava flows forming the island continued until June 5, 1967. Since then, the sea and wind have **eroded** the parts of the island that were made from loosely packed volcanic **debris**. However, lava that flowed over much of the island created enough solid rock to make sure that Surtsey will be around for at least another 100 years.

Many kinds of scientists were excited about the formation of this new piece of land. Geologists could see and study firsthand the kinds of things that happened billions of years ago when the earth itself was first formed. **Botanists** and **biologists** were interested in when and how plants and animals would colonize the bare rock and sand of the new island. Over the years, they have carefully monitored each new species of moss, grass, insect, and bird that has made Surtsey its new home.

STOP AND THINK

1. Are the last two sentences in the final entry in the ship's log fact or opinion?

2. Why were geologists so eager to study Surtsey Island?

185

CULTURAL CONNECTION

Wyoming

A TOWER OF STONE

FOCUS: How can a legend help explain the changing earth?

Devils Tower is a huge rock column rising 865 feet up into the Wyoming sky. The tower is imposing and **dramatic**, but the way it sticks straight up is also rather spooky and strange. Maybe that's how it got its name. In any case, every year about 450,000 people make the trip to see this national monument.

Geologists can explain how the tower was formed. First, an ancient volcano forced hot magma up into a pocket in the earth. Then the magma cooled and became rock. Over time, wind and water eroded much rock and earth around the column. The rock column was left standing, high and all alone.

Crow, Kiowa, Sioux, and other American Indians share a story about the origin of Devils Tower. Below is a version of the legend for you to read. If you ever have the chance to visit Wyoming, see if you can spot the "bear scratches" along the sides of the column. What do they look like to you?

It was full summer and much too hot in the sun! Their band was camped a little way up the stream. They came to this place for the chokecherries every year. Now the berries were almost ripe, and soon the girls and their mothers would go out to gather them in their harvest baskets. But not quite yet! Today, they were still free to do as they wished. The girls found a nice cool patch of shade under a cottonwood tree. They sat down to rest and began to tell each other stories.

◀ **Devils Tower National Monument, Wyoming, U.S.A.**

187

"Once upon a time there was a big, terrible bear with smelly yellow claws who loved to eat little girls," started Heavy Cloud.

"Oh, don't talk about bears!" said Willow Dancer. "There are too many of them around here. Don't scare us."

"Nonsense," replied Heavy Cloud. "We shouldn't be afraid of any bear. We can always run away."

"Yes, but some bears run very fast," said Willow Dancer. "They make *me* scared."

"Shh," whispered Red Spotted Deer. "I think I hear something in the bushes."

The girls were quiet and listened. There was **definitely** a rustling. Suddenly, the rustling started getting louder, faster, and closer! The girls jumped to their feet, but it was already too late. That very second, a huge bear burst from the bushes, chasing toward them at a terrible speed. It was the biggest, meanest-looking bear the girls had ever seen.

"Run!" shouted Heavy Cloud. "Run for home!"

The girls ran toward the stream and down the bank, then splashed across the sandy streambed. The bear was right behind them, grunting and growling as it ran. The girls scrambled up the other bank and headed out across a stretch of sand and stones. The bear was getting closer every second. Any second now they expected to feel its sharp, yellow claws tearing into their backs.

They could see the teepees of their home camp in the distance, and the bear was too close. They were never going to make it! Just ahead was a rock about three feet high, with just room enough on top for all seven girls. Without even thinking, the girls jumped up on the rock. It was not high enough to keep them safe from the bear, but they had run out of choices. There was nothing left to do but huddle together and pray.

"Rock, save us!" cried Heavy Cloud. "Keep us from the bear."

"Yes," prayed Willow Dancer, Red Spotted Deer, and the others. "We beg you. Save us!"

188

The rock heard their prayers and cries and had pity on them. All of a sudden, it started to grow. It grew higher and higher, with the girls **clinging** to each other on top. The bear roared with anger. It stood on its hind legs and scratched at the sides of the rock, trying to reach the girls. It circled the rock, leaving long scratch marks on every side. But the rock was too tall. The bear could not reach the girls. They were safe.

The angry bear headed back to the forest, growling and grunting all the way. But the rock kept on growing, pushing higher and higher up into the sky. How could the girls come down?

They couldn't. It was impossible. Instead, they rose up into the sky and became a group of seven bright stars called the Pleiades. In the middle of the night in wintertime, you can see this group of stars right over the tall rock. The seven girls are still there, shining brightly to thank the rock for saving them from the claws of the angry bear.

STOP AND THINK

1. What was the effect of wind and water erosion around the column of rock?

2. Why do you think American Indians created this legend?

UNIT 8 AMAZING POWERS

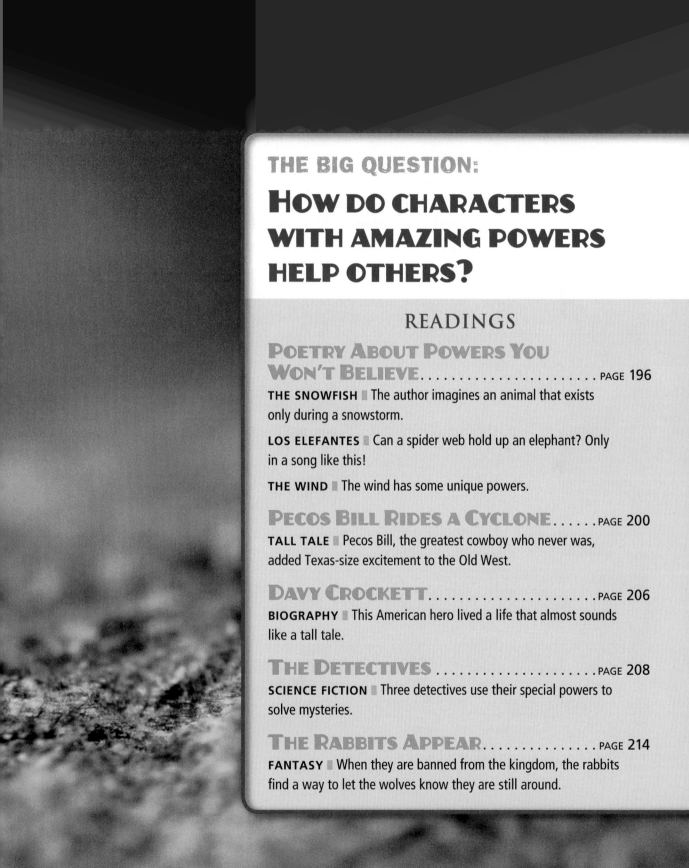

AMAZING POWERS

In what types of literature can you find people with superpowers?

You can find people with superpowers in...

- ☐ comic books.
- ☐ folktales.
- ☐ myths.
- ☐ science fiction.

What amazing deeds can people do in real life?

In real life, people can...

- ☐ ride a cyclone.
- ☐ explore the wilderness alone.
- ☐ carry their weight in wildcats.
- ☐ find enough food to keep a small army fed.

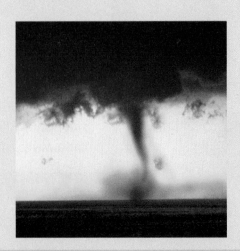

What are some things you'd expect to find in a science fiction story?

In a science fiction story I would expect to find...

- ☐ unusual ways for people to communicate.

- ☐ plots that seem incredible.

- ☐ characters with unusual powers.

- ☐ vehicles that use new technology.

In literature, what do people with amazing powers do?

In literature, people with amazing powers...

- ☐ challenge a villain.

- ☐ solve a mystery.

- ☐ help people or communities in distress.

- ☐ use their power to win contests.

When an evil ruler threatens people, how can they show their strength?

When an evil ruler threatens people, they can show their strength by...

- ☐ protesting.

- ☐ moving somewhere else.

- ☐ quietly defying the ruler.

- ☐ getting outside help.

Literature Words

actual

cannery

claim

denial

excuse

ragged

restlessness

stake

waltz

youth

---

actual

Actual means real and existing as a fact.

66 The TV program was based on an actual event in history. 99

---

cannery

A **cannery** is a factory where food such as meat, fish, or fruit is canned.

66 My brother works at the fish cannery. 99

---

ragged

Ragged means worn out, uneven, or shaggy.

66 The winter coat was ragged around the edges. 99

---

restlessness

Restlessness refers to the inability to relax or be still.

66 His restlessness was due to the long train ride. 99

claim

A **claim** is an established or recognized right.

" The farming family had a claim on the land by the river. **"**

denial

A **denial** is a refusal to believe or accept something.

" He repeated his denial that he owed me an apology. **"**

excuse

An **excuse** is an inferior or poor example of something.

" That blurred photo is a poor excuse for a picture. **"**

stake

Stake means to take, claim, or reserve a share of land.

" During a land rush, families can stake a claim to a plot of land. **"**

waltz

A **waltz** is a ballroom dance.

" The prince and princess danced a waltz at their wedding. **"**

youth

Youth refers to the time of being young.

" The old pictures reminded the woman of her youth. **"**

FROM

THE SNOWFISH

BY EDWARD FIELD

As oceans are to porpoises
The snowdrift to the snowfish is.
The snowfish swims down with the snow
And tunnels in the drifts below.

Some creatures move in air or mud,
Moles in earth and worms in wood,
Owls in **hollow** trunks of trees:
Many the shapes of nature's fancies.

His **various** fishy cousins swim
In water for a **medium**.
These he **resembles** more or less
In iridescent nakedness.

Little about him can be taught
By scientific schools of thought.
He does not seem to fit the rules
That work for those who swim in schools.

And though great numbers of him fall
The snowfish won't **conform** at all.
The photograph you try to take
Will melt him quicker than a snowflake.

You cannot catch him with a line:
When thickets of snow are coming down
You know the snowfish is around
By the knocking on your windowblind. . .

Los elefantes
(The Elephant Song)

One elephant balanced
On the web of a spider.
When he saw that it held him up,
He called another elephant.

Two elephants balanced
On the web of a spider.
When they saw that it held them up,
They called another elephant.

Three elephants balanced
On the web of a spider.
When they saw that it held them up,
They called another elephant.

*—From a traditional song
translated by Ubaldo Feliciano*

THE WIND

BY JAMES REEVES

I can go through a doorway without any key,
And strip the leaves from the great oak tree.

I can drive storm-clouds and shake tall towers,
Or steal through a garden and not wake the flowers.

Seas I can move and ships I can sink;
I can carry a house-top or the scent of a pink.

When I am angry, I can rave and riot;
And when I am spent, I lie quiet as quiet.

Comprehension

✓ **TARGET SKILL** **Author's Motive** The reason an author writes is called the author's motive. Authors of stories often write to entertain or to share their own feelings about life. Sometimes they write to teach a lesson about life. Figuring out the author's motive can help you better understand a story.

Here is an excerpt from "The Trunk." It is the story of a Japanese-American girl named Rinko growing up in the 1930s. One afternoon, Rinko learns something about her past and about her Japanese heritage that she had not known before.

From what Mama says and does, you can tell that she thinks of the young girl she once was as someone who no longer exists, or someone who exists only in the old photographs in the trunk.

One afternoon when Mama and I were down in the basement trying to get rid of some empty cartons and old newspapers, Mama came across the big trunk she'd brought with her from Japan. I'd never seen her open it up, so I asked if there was anything inside.

"Oh, yes," Mama said. "My Japanese self."

I didn't know what Mama meant until she blew off the dust on top and lifted the heavy lid of the trunk . . .

She showed me her school notebooks filled with feathery writing in faced dust-colored ink. And she showed me lots of photographs . . .

Mama got very quiet then, and she put everything back in the tray, giving each album a little pat as she put it down. Then she closed the lid and gave that a few pats, too, as though she was saying good-bye to everything inside.

I stayed in the basement for a while though, because I had a lot of thoughts muddling around in my head. I felt as if Mama wasn't just plain Mama anymore. It was as if part of her was locked up in her big trunk, never able to get out.

Though the story is fiction, it is very realistic. Rinko's mother is American, but she was born in Japan. In this passage, she deals with her "Japanese self" by keeping it closed away in a trunk. Rinko, who shares this Japanese heritage, is naturally curious about her mother's early life.

The author's motive is first to entertain. She also wants to show a unique challenge that people have who belong to two cultures. Many people who live in two cultures choose to express both cultures in their lives. Mama, however, seems to have laid aside her Japanese past.

You can use this graphic organizer to keep track of story clues related to the characters and the plot. Thinking about the clues can help you understand the author's motive.

Clues	Authors Motive
Rinko has never seen what is in the trunk.	
Rinko's mother says that her Japanese self is in the trunk.	
Her mother shows her lots of old photographs.	
Her mother gets very quiet and closes the lid of the trunk.	
She pats the lid as if she is saying goodbye to all the memories inside.	
Rinko sees her mother in a different way but is not exactly sure of her own feelings.	The author writes very realistically. She wants readers to understand the emotions that the characters in the story are feeling.

✓ **TARGET STRATEGY** **Analyze/Evaluate** Some stories are meant both to entertain and to describe realistically something special about life. As you read these kinds of stories, you can use clues about characters and their actions to infer the theme of the story. Ask yourself the following questions:

• What are the main characters doing?

• What are the characters feeling?

• How do characters feel about one another?

• What does the story seem to be about?

Tall tales are stories of men and women who are larger than life. These imaginary **characters** perform amazing feats of strength and show great daring and cunning. They are bigger, faster, and smarter than anyone else. They **succeed** with ease when everyone else fails.

Many tall tales are told about life on the American frontier. Pecos Bill is a favorite hero of the Southwest. He was the greatest cowboy ever. He blazed around Texas on his horse, Lightning. He was said to have invented many of the most important parts of cowboy life, for example the lasso, branding, and bucking broncos.

PECOS BILL
RIDES A CYCLONE

By Mia Lewis,
adapted from Pecos Bill tall tales

Pecos Bill's parents were heading west. They didn't notice when one of their eighteen children fell with a thump out of their crowded covered wagon near the Pecos River.

Little Bill was adopted by an old and wise coyote. He grew up believing himself a full-blooded member of the pack. He ran, hunted, howled at the moon, and spoke Coyote with the best of them. Years later, a passing stranger told him he was not a coyote but a person!

When Pecos Bill discovered he was a human, there was nothing for him to do but become a cowboy. He scared the skin off a steer and made himself some clothes. Then he set off to find the ranch with the toughest cowboys in all of Texas. When his horse gave out, he fought a mountain lion and rode that instead.

Arriving on the big cat, with a 50-foot rattlesnake round his wrist, Bill asked the cowboys around the fire who was boss.

"I used to be," said the biggest cowboy there, "but now you are."

"Good," said Bill. "Now, let's do some ranching!"

201

But the house on Mango Street is not the way they told it at all. It's small and red with tight steps in front and windows so small you'd think they were holding their breath. Bricks are crumbling in places, and the front door is so swollen you have to push hard to get in. There is no front yard, only four little elms the city planted by the curb. Out back is a small garage for the car we don't own yet and a small backyard that looks smaller between the two buildings on either side. There are stairs in our house, but they're ordinary hallway stairs, and the house has only one washroom. Everybody has to share a bedroom—Mama and Papa, Carlos and Kiki, me and Nenny.

Once when we were living on Loomis, a nun from my school passed by and saw me playing out front. The laundromat downstairs had been boarded up because it had been robbed two days before and the owner had painted on the wood YES WE'RE OPEN so as not to lose business.

Where do you live? she asked.

There, I said pointing up to the third floor.

You live *there?*

There. I had to look to where she pointed—the third floor, the paint peeling, wooden bars Papa had nailed on the windows so we wouldn't fall out. You live *there?* The way she said it made me feel like nothing. *There.* I lived *there.* I nodded.

I knew then I had to have a house. A real house. One I could point to. But this isn't it. The house on Mango Street isn't it. For the time being, Mama says. Temporary, says Papa. But I know how those things go.

Four trees planted by the city on Esperanza's block are far more meaningful to her because nature is rare on Mango Street.

They are the only ones who understand me. I am the only one who understands them. Four skinny trees with skinny necks and pointy elbows like mine. Four who do not belong here but are here. Four **raggedy excuses** planted by the city. From our room we can hear them, but Nenny just sleeps and doesn't appreciate these things.

Their strength is secret. They send ferocious roots beneath the ground. They grow up and they grow down and grab the earth between their hairy toes and bite the sky with violent teeth and never quit their anger. This is how they keep.

Let one forget his reason for being, they'd all droop like tulips in a glass, each with its arms around the other. Keep, keep, keep, trees say when I sleep. They teach.

When I am too sad and too skinny to keep keeping, when I am a tiny thing against so many bricks, then it is I look at trees. When there is nothing left to look at on this street. Four who grew despite concrete. Four who reach and do not forget to reach. Four whose only reason is to be and be.

STOP AND THINK

1. Why does Esperanza seem to value the trees on her block?

2. How can something you hope for or dream of have value?

203

Your Turn

Use Your Words:

assault	hunch
bewilder	ideal
cease	insolent
character	margin
comply	nestle
concept	nuclear
distribute	occasional
element	style
epidemic	suited
frolic	supreme

- Read the words on the list.
- Read the dialogue. Find the words.

Look, the city is building a new-style nuclear power plant. They say it's an ideal spot.

It will be nestled by those trees near the river. Everyone has to comply with the decision.

Not me. I'm insolent. That spot isn't suited for a nuclear plant.

I have a hunch that there will be occasional accidents.

And epidemics.

MORE ACTIVITIES

1. Take a Survey

Graphic Organizer

What type of energy or power do your classmates prefer? Ask 12 classmates to choose among the types of energy and power listed below. Tally their answers. Share your findings with your class.

2. Make a Flyer

Speaking and Listening

Make a flyer protesting the building of a nuclear power plant. Show your flyer to your partner. Share your ideas about the nuclear power plant.

Nuclear energy	Solar energy	Wind power	Oil and gas power	Electric power

3. What's Your Hunch?
Writing

Have you ever had a hunch about something? Write a paragraph telling about your hunch. Share your paragraph with a partner.

4. Make a List
Vocabulary

A birthday is an occasional happening. With a partner, list other occasional happenings. Share your list with your class.

5. Play "Who Am I?"
Speaking and Listening

Choose a person in the picture. A partner asks five yes-or-no questions to guess the person. Then change places with your partner.

6. What's Your Style?
Vocabulary and writing

List ten words that describe your own style. The words can describe the way you dress, talk, or act. Use the words to write a poem about yourself.

205

The Race for Land

From *Pappy's Handkerchief*
by Devin Scillian
illustrated by Chris Ellison

FOCUS: What hardships are people willing to endure to acquire a home they can call their own?

Moses, *a young African American boy, lives in Baltimore in 1889. His family, who is going through tough times, hears about farmland that will be available in Indian Territory, also called Oklahoma. There is to be a land rush—an* **actual** *race during which people can* **stake** *a* **claim** *to a* **plot** *of free farmland—on April 22. The family—including Moses' parents, his grandparents Granny and Pappy, and his siblings James, Virginia, Lacy, and Noah—head west to take part in the land rush. Traveling with them is a friend, Liberty, whose ability to read and write is a real help on the journey. The family's wagon, pulled by the horses Rumble and Maybelle, rolls on despite many difficulties, including illness.*

On Saturday, April 20th, we arrived at a camp in Indian Territory near a town called Kingfisher. We had arrived just in time. We were running low on food. The trip had been hard on Maybelle and she was beginning to limp. And while little Noah was feeling better, the fever had now moved on to Pappy. He lay in the back of the wagon and told us not to worry and that he would be ready for Monday morning.

There were people and horses and wagons and mules everywhere, camped along a line of white stakes stretching across the flat Oklahoma plains. The horizon had never seemed so far away. Soldiers rode between the campfires explaining the rules for the run and warning us about straying across the **boundary** line too soon. And sure enough, every so often, soldiers would ride in from the boundary line with a cheater under arrest.

The Detectives

From *The Ear, the Eye, and the Arm* by Nancy Farmer

FOCUS: What special powers might be helpful to detectives?

This science fiction selection is set in the African country of Zimbabwe in the year 2194—almost two centuries into the future. The action begins in the office of a detective agency located in a dangerous suburb called the Cow's Guts. A mother is calling the detectives to ask for help in finding her missing children.

In case you haven't thought about the far future before, you'll need to know that a holophone and a holoscreen show three-dimensional images, and an antigrav (antigravity) unit adjusts the ground's gravitational pull so that an airborne vehicle can take off or land.

When the holophone rang at the Ear, the Eye and the Arm Detective Agency, all three men sprang to answer it. Arm won, as he always did. His long black snaky arm far outreached anyone else's. Besides, the tips of his fingers were slightly sticky.

"Hello! Detective agency. You lose 'em, we find 'em," he cried. Ear folded his sensitive ears, and a look of pain crossed his face.

"Sorry," said Arm, lowering his voice.

"I—I need your help," said Mother on the holoscreen.

"You came to the right place," Arm said. "Nobody else can do what we do. We can hear a bat burp in the basement. We can see a gnat's navel on a foggy night. Hunches stick to us like gum to your shoe."

Mother introduces herself as the wife of General Amadeus Matsika, the country's security chief.

"I can't explain on the phone," said Mother. "If you're not busy, could I send the stretch limo to pick you up? Please don't be busy," she added with a tremor Arm picked up at once.

"At your service. We'll rearrange our appointments," the detective said graciously.

"Oh, thank you," Mother cried. She hung up.

The men smiled at one another. The area in front of the holophone showed a desk neatly piled with papers, a **swivel** chair and what appeared to be a diploma on the wall. Close up, the diploma turned out to be a gift certificate. Just out of holoscreen range were a sink full of dirty dishes, a **muddle** of food containers and a sagging couch.

"Do you want me to rearrange the appointments?" said Eye. Arm nodded, so Eye took down the calendar and erased *Take clothes to laundry* and wrote in *Important case for General Matsika* instead.

"She didn't ask how much we charged. That's always a good sign," remarked Ear.

"But what can Matsika want that he can't get?" Arm said. "He can call in the police, the army and the secret service. If he says 'boo,' a mugger at the other end of the city drops a wallet."

Eye fitted on dark glasses in preparation for going outside. "Perhaps it's a question of being too powerful."

Granny made sure Pappy and Liberty were low in the wagon and pulled James, Virginia, and Lacy close to her. Ma held Noah tightly in her arms. And we waited.

Suddenly, a cannon fired from the east, a **thunderous** BOOM that sent half the horses **rearing** back on their hind legs. But in a huge cloud of dust, the swarm of settlers dashed into the land that looked so golden and precious from our camps. Those on single horses raced way out in front and quickly disappeared on the far horizon. The very first wagons across the line only had to travel a few hundred yards to stake claims on the first acres up for grabs. But they were nearly run over as they tried to stop on their new homestead with so many others having to charge through to stake the next claim.

We had to wait a few minutes for the wagons in front of us to get on their way, but finally Rumble and Maybelle surged across the line amid the whoops and hollers of the thousands of settlers around us. The land before us finally opened up and we were dashing along with a stiff Oklahoma wind in our faces. But long gone were the smooth trails of well-traveled country. Indian Territory was covered in deep **ruts** and **culverts** and our wagon began to bounce furiously across the ditches. Liberty's head hit hard on the floor of the wagon, and James and Lacy were crying because they were so afraid.

The deep grass hid the dry creek bed ahead of us. We never saw it, and neither did Maybelle as she stumbled forward on her bad leg and lost her footing. She tumbled down and the wagon jerked violently to her side. Pa tried to pull back on Rumble's **rein**, but suddenly the front wheel bounced down into the culvert and as Maybelle fell, the wagon bounced hard into the air and smashed back to the ground. Pa and I flew off the buckboard and into the grass. Rumble was down, too, and both horses whinnied in pain.

The accident has damaged the wagon and injured Maybelle the horse. Worst of all, Pa's leg is broken when he tries to lift the wagon to free Maybelle. It looks as though the race for land is over for the family.

But Pappy, looking weak and **haggard**, let out a loud groan. He raised himself from the grass and looked out across the Oklahoma plain and turned to me.

"Moses," he said, "It's up to you."

I had no idea what he meant. But he reached into his pocket and drew out a white handkerchief.

"You take Rumble," he said. "You ride like the wind, as far and as fast as you can. And when you find our farm, you bury this handkerchief in the ground and you claim it as ours."

I expected someone to protest. But as I looked to my father, I could see that he was already trying to reach over to **unharness** Rumble.

211

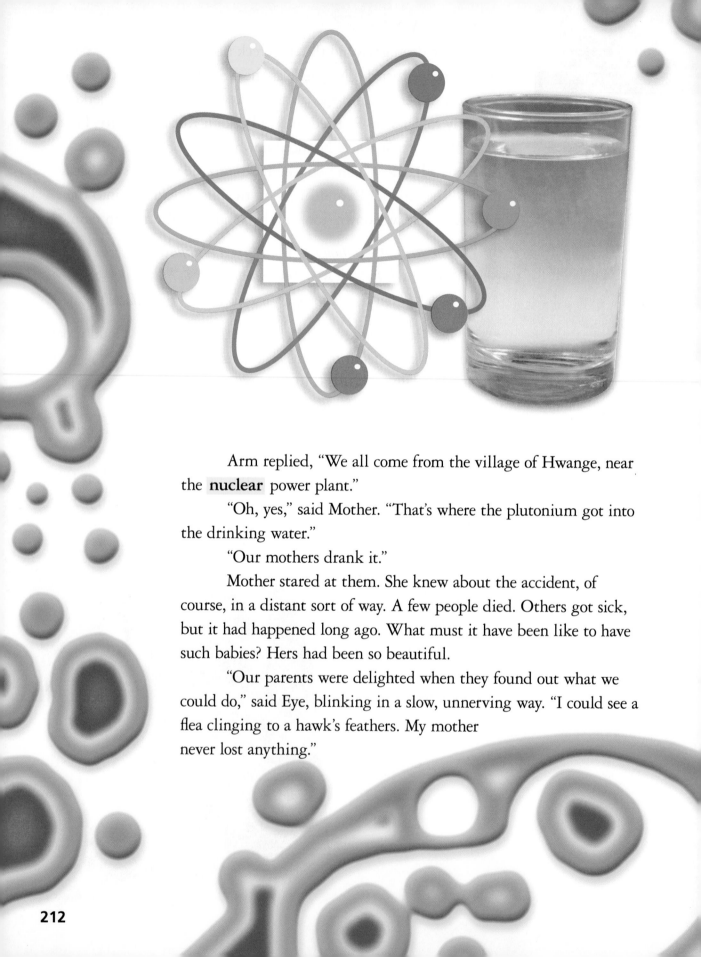

Arm replied, "We all come from the village of Hwange, near the **nuclear** power plant."

"Oh, yes," said Mother. "That's where the plutonium got into the drinking water."

"Our mothers drank it."

Mother stared at them. She knew about the accident, of course, in a distant sort of way. A few people died. Others got sick, but it had happened long ago. What must it have been like to have such babies? Hers had been so beautiful.

"Our parents were delighted when they found out what we could do," said Eye, blinking in a slow, unnerving way. "I could see a flea clinging to a hawk's feathers. My mother never lost anything."

"I could hear an ant creeping up on the sugar bowl," boasted Ear.

"And what could you do?" said Mother, **bewildered** by these strange creatures.

"I got **hunches**," Arm said. "I used to know when the baboons were planning to raid the fields. So you see, we were **ideally suited** to become detectives."

"Who are these people?" growled Father from the doorway. Ear closed his ears at once. Arm staggered back as though struck.

"Detectives," Mother replied. "They're going to look for the children."

The detectives track the children through many dangerous places. Thanks to their amazing powers, as well as their courage, the detectives help rescue the children in the end.

The **concept** of heroes with superhuman abilities started centuries ago, in myths and folktales from countless cultures around the globe. Today, heroes with spectacular powers can be found in tall tales, futuristic science fiction stories, comic books, and special effects-filled action movies.

STOP AND THINK

1. Which of the detectives seems to have more than one unusual power? Explain.

2. What amazing ability would you like to have? Why?

The Trunk

From *A Jar of Dreams*
by Yoshiko Uchida

FOCUS: What can a person's belongings tell you about that person?

Rinko was born in the United States, but her parents come from Japan. In the Depression of the 1930s it's hard for the family to make money, and they also have to deal with racism. Yet there's a lot to enjoy in life, including the upcoming visit of Rinko's aunt. Aunt Waka, Mama's sister, is coming from Japan to spend some time with the family in California. The family works hard to prepare for this honored guest. As Rinko and Mama clean, they come upon something that was once very important to Mama.

One afternoon when Mama and I were down in the basement trying to get rid of some empty cartons and old newspapers, Mama came across the big **trunk** she'd brought with her from Japan. I'd never seen her open it up, so I asked if there was anything inside.

"Oh, yes," Mama said. "My Japanese self."

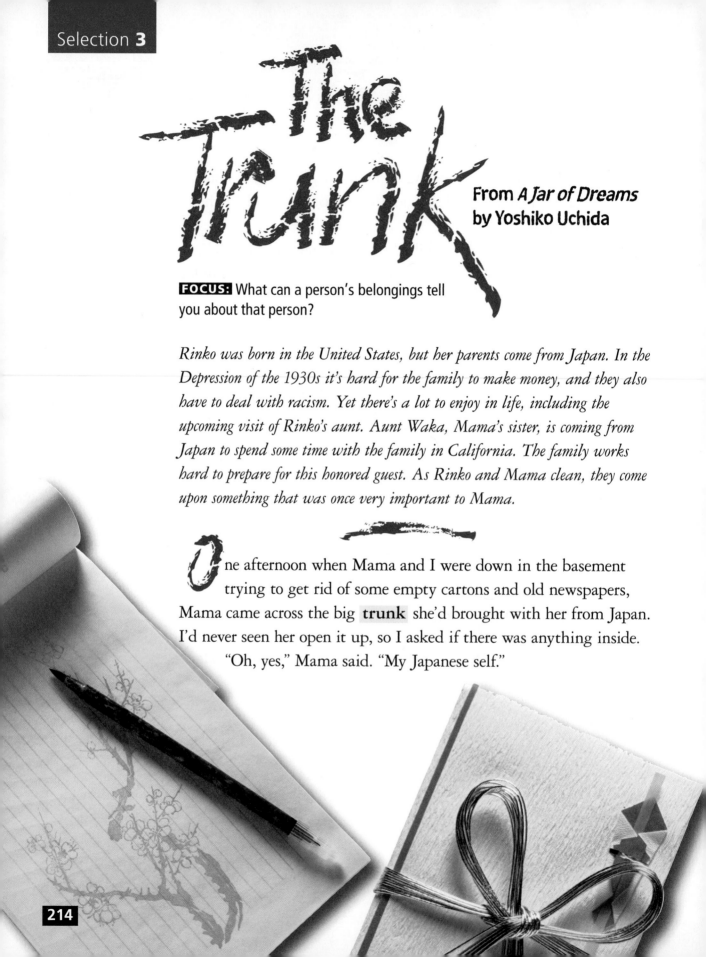

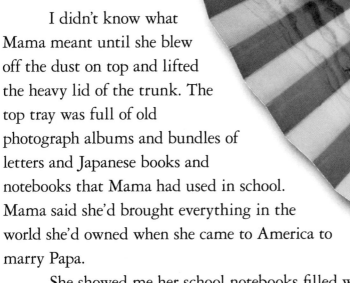

I didn't know what Mama meant until she blew off the dust on top and lifted the heavy lid of the trunk. The top tray was full of old photograph albums and bundles of letters and Japanese books and notebooks that Mama had used in school. Mama said she'd brought everything in the world she'd owned when she came to America to marry Papa.

She showed me her school notebooks filled with feathery writing in **faded** dust-colored ink. And she showed me lots of photographs. One was of her family. There were Grandpa and Grandma looking younger than I'd ever seen them, my two uncles wearing school uniforms, and Mama and Aunt Waka when they were twelve and thirteen. Aunt Waka was standing with a crutch, and Mama told me she'd had to use a crutch for a long time because she'd been born with a **deformed** foot. But Aunt Waka didn't look sad about it. In fact, she was the only one in the photo who was smiling. Everybody else looked so solemn, they almost seemed sad. But Mama said picture-taking was serious business in those days.

The King of the Wolves was not in the best of moods when the monkey came in. "You're late. And I'm in a hurry. I need photographs of each important act in my life. And all my acts, let me tell you, are **supremely** important. . . . Can you guess what we're going to do with those pictures? You can't? We're going to put one on every street, inside every bush, in every home. I'll be there, watching each citizen with my very own eyes. You'd better pity those who don't have the latest events in my life hung up on their walls. And you know who is going to **distribute** each picture? You don't know?"

The monkey was trembling so hard that no words came out.

"The birds, ugly monkey. Now they'll bite their own beaks before they twitter around with any nonsense about rabbits. And we'll tie an endless cord to their legs, so they can't escape. Understand?"

The monkey understood so well that his trembling paw immediately clicked the shutter of the camera, taking the first picture.

"Go," roared the Wolf, "and develop it. I want it on every wall in the kingdom."

But when the photographer returned some minutes later, he did not dare enter the throne room, and asked one of the soldiers to call the counselor. Without a word, the monkey passed him the picture he had just taken.

The fox blinked once, and then blinked again. In the corner of the photo, far from the muscular, ferocious figure of the King—who had both arms up in the air as if he had just won a boxing championship—appeared what was without any doubt the beginning of an ear, the ear of someone who had **insolently** come to spy on the whole ceremony.

"You blind monkey!" fumed the fox. "How come you didn't notice that this . . . this thing was there? Can't you focus that camera of yours?"

"If it could get into the picture," the monkey answered, "it was because you and your guards let it get close."

"It won't happen again," the counselor promised. "Rub out that . . . ear before His Wolfishness finds out."

From his bag, the monkey took out a special liquid that he used to erase any detail that might bother a client. The intruding ear began to disappear as if it had never existed.

The King of Wolves was pleased with the portrait and ordered it sent all over the realm. Two hours later, he personally went on an inspection tour to make sure that not a window was without a picture of his large, gleaming, dangerous grin. "Not bad," he said, "but this photo is already getting old. People should see my latest deeds. Take another. Quick. Show me scaring pigeons—right away. And bring it to me immediately. You took too long last time."

But the monkey wasn't able to **comply** this time, either. Once again he had the counselor called secretly.

"Again?" asked the fox. "It happened again?"

Except that now it was worse than an indiscreet ear. The whole corner of the picture was filled with the unmistakable face of . . . yes, there was no denying it, of a rabbit winking an eye in open defiance of the nearby guards.

UNIT

9 THEY LED THE WAY

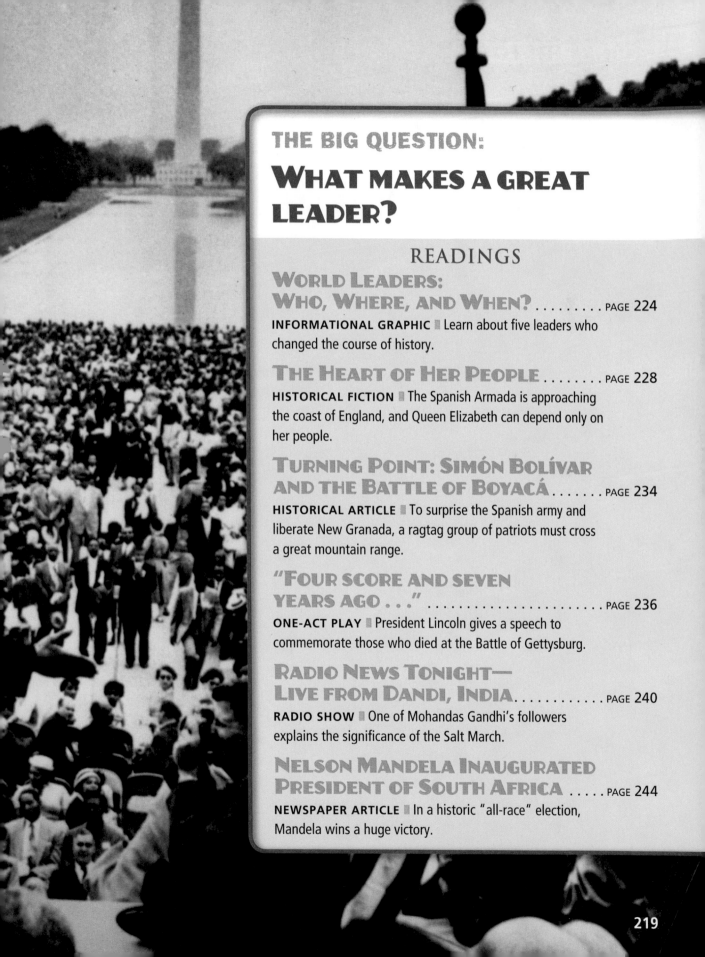

THE BIG QUESTION:

WHAT MAKES A GREAT LEADER?

READINGS

UNIT 9 ROAD TO CIVILIZATION

LEARN THE WORDS

History Words

adjust

assassinate

feeble

garment

inflame

liberate

magnificent

maneuver

nationality

resolution

---

adjust

To **adjust** is to move something into position or make it comfortable.

66 You can adjust the car seat if a taller person sits in it. 99

---

assassinate

To **assassinate** is to murder, usually for political or religious reasons.

66 John Wilkes Booth, a Confederate sympathizer, assassinated President Lincoln. 99

---

liberate

To **liberate** is to set free, as from opression or foreign control.

66 George Washington helped liberate the American colonies from English rule. 99

---

magnificent

Magnificent means very impressive or beautiful.

66 The oak tree, well over 400 years old, is magnificent. 99

feeble

Feeble means lacking in strength or vigor.

“ The plant was feeble because it got no sunlight. ”

garment

A **garment** is a piece of clothing.

“ She threw her garments in a suitcase and rushed to the airport. ”

inflame

To **inflame** is to arouse strong emotions.

“ News of the crime inflamed the public's wrath. ”

maneuver

To **maneuver** is to make a series of movements to gain an advantage.

“ Under heavy fire, the battalion maneuvered to secure the hilltop. ”

nationality

Nationality is the condition of belonging to a particular nation.

“ Our grandfather is proud of his Polish nationality. ”

resolution

Resolution is firmness of purpose.

“ In the face of heated criticism, the governor showed resolution and refused to back down. ”

History Words

attest

capital

cylinder

edible

preserve

remains

site

strategy

symbol

vein

attest

Attest means to bear witness, or to declare to be correct or true.

66 I attest that the package contains no liquids. 99

capital

A **capital** is the city or town that is the seat of government.

66 Washington, D.C., is the capital of the United States. 99

remains

Remains refers to all that is left after other objects are used up, destroyed, or taken away.

66 When we arrived, we saw the remains of the ancient village. 99

site

Site refers to the position or location of a town or building.

66 The site of the ancient city was on a river bank. 99

cylinder

A **cylinder** is a barrel-shaped curved solid.

❝ Writing was etched into the surface of the clay cylinder. ❞

edible

Edible means fit to be eaten as food.

❝ The guide book said the wild red berries were edible. ❞

preserve

Preserve means to keep up or maintain.

❝ We will preserve the ancient ruins. ❞

strategy

A **strategy** is a plan or method used to attain a specific goal.

❝ John had a good strategy when it came to studying for a test. ❞

symbol

A **symbol** is something used for, or representing, something else.

❝ The bald eagle is a symbol of our nation. ❞

vein

A **vein** is a long strip of igneous rock or mineral that fills a crevice in another rock.

❝ She could see a vein of gold in the rock. ❞

Comprehension

✔ **TARGET SKILL** **Problem/Solution** Writers of informational articles often tell about problems and how the problems are solved. The writers may tell about one problem or several related problems. Sometimes one problem will have several solutions. Other times several problems will have the same solution.

Here is an example of two related problems and their solutions:

Born in 1918, Nelson Mandela grew up in rural South Africa. White South Africans ruled the country, and black South Africans suffered discrimination in all aspects of their lives. When Mandela was in his 30s, South Africa adopted an official policy of racial separation called apartheid. Mandela's battles against apartheid would put him in prison beginning in 1962...

Mandela was an international symbol of the injustice of apartheid. All over the world, people demanded, "Free Mandela!"...

When President de Klerk took office in 1989, negotiations began for South Africa's political future. Mandela was released in February 1990. The two men continued to work together to find a way to end apartheid. In 1993, they won the Nobel Peace Prize for their efforts.

Problem
South Africa adopted an official policy of racial separation.

Problem
Nelson Mandela was put in prison in 1962.

Solution
People around the world demanded that Mandela be freed.

Solution
President de Klerk of South Africa and Mandela worked together to end racial separation

Solution
Mandela was released from prison in 1990.

You can use a graphic organizer to show problems and solutions.

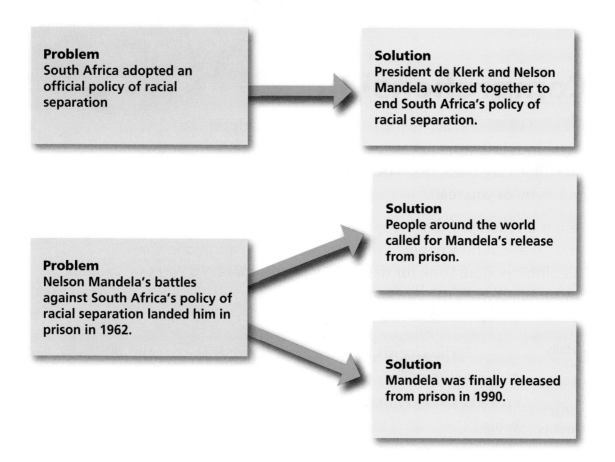

The boxes on the left show two related problems. The boxes on the right show the solutions to the problems. Notice that two arrows from the second box on the left point to solutions on the right. This shows that several things happened to help solve the problem.

✔ TARGET STRATEGY Summarize You can use a problem/solution graphic organizer to help you summarize an article. Remember, a summary should contain only the most important ideas and relevant details. The major problems and their solutions mentioned in an article are important ideas. You should include them in your summary.

Comprehension

✓ **TARGET SKILL** **Description** Writers use description to explain what things look like, what things are made of, and how things are used. Good descriptions help you see things in your mind as you read.

Here is an excerpt from "People of the Stone Age." It tells a little bit about how people lived thousands of years ago in the Paleolithic period. Look for descriptive details that help you see in your mind what the author is talking about.

> These details show the different kinds of remains that archaeologists examine.

Archaeologists are scientists who study the remains of earlier cultures. They examine things such as graves, artwork, and tools to understand the people who left them behind. . .

We know that Paleolithic people had fire because archaeologists have found burned animal bones at sites dating from those times. The ability to control fire was an important step forward. . .

> This description helps you see a cave painting in France. Think what the walls of those caves must look like!

The cave paintings made by Paleolithic people show how important animals were to them. One cave in Lascaux, France, shows a few stick-figure people, no plants, and about 600 paintings of animals.

> These details can help you see in your mind the colors used in a cave painting. It helps you understand how painters used natural materials.

Paleolithic artists often used different-colored clays or earth for their paintings. They also used wood charcoal for black. Chalk, bone, or shell made white. Stones with mineral veins gave them red and yellow.

You can use this graphic organizer to keep track of story clues that help you understand the author's motive.

Objects or How Things Were Used **Description**

| the remains of earlier cultures | → | graves, artwork, tools, burned animal bones |

| cave paintings | → | a few stick-figure people

no plants

about 600 paintings of animals. |

| how Paleolithic artists worked | → | painted with different-colored clay or earth

used wood charcoal for black

used chalk, bone, or shells for white

used mineral veins in stones for red and yellow |

✔ **TARGET STRATEGY** **Questions** Asking and answering questions as you read can help you better understand and remember what you are reading. Ask questions such as the following:

- What is this article mainly about?

- What can I learn from this article?
- Which details help me see in my mind what I am reading about?
- What things don't I understand? Where can I go back to check on things I don't quite understand?

A knight riding to a tournament—combat stage as a sport—during Elizabeth's reign

Queen Elizabeth I never married, but she had many proposals. She had many suitors, including princes and kings from powerful foreign lands. Elizabeth protected England's interests by keeping all of them guessing. "I am already bound unto a husband," she said, "which is the Kingdom of England."

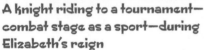

LOOK IT UP

For more on Queen Elizabeth I:
Good Queen Bess, Tudor Dynasty,
Elizabethan Era

ruler for 30 years, but they still thought of her as their magnificent Faerie Queen.

"My loving people," she called to the troops, "I have placed my chiefest strength and safeguard in the loyal hearts and good will of my subjects…I am resolved to lay down my life for my God and for my kingdom and for my people …I know I have the body of a weak and **feeble** woman, but I have the heart and the stomach of a king." It was becoming difficult to hear her words over the roar of cheers for "good Queen Bess." Gazing proudly over the throng, she finished, "We shall shortly have a famous victory over those enemies of my God, of my kingdom, and of my people."

As the Earl of Leicester watched Elizabeth inspire the soldiers with her **resolution**, he could only shake his head in wonderment. Surely she had so **inflamed** their spirits that the weakest among them could now match any Spaniard that dared land on English soil. "I worry that you are so near the coast," he told her, as they rode back to her lodging. "What if a raiding party from the armada has come ashore?" King Philip, they both knew, would like nothing more than to capture Elizabeth as a war prize.

"I have no fear," Elizabeth said, her head high. At that moment, they saw a cloud of dust on the road leading from the coast. And then a rider appeared, galloping toward them.

"It is the royal messenger," said Leicester, "with word of the battle." He and the queen reined in their horses as the messenger rushed toward them.

"They have fled," the messenger gasped. "We have overpowered their ships with our own. And God has sent a mighty wind that has pushed them north toward Scotland. They are gone, your Majesty!"

Elizabeth looked at Leicester. She said nothing, but her heart filled with pride. Her English navy had defeated the mighty armada of Spain.

For months, England celebrated the victory. All across the land, there were holidays, bonfires, and church services. In November, Elizabeth rode through crowded London streets in an open carriage, cheered the entire way. Inside St. Paul's Church, she knelt beneath banners captured from the Spanish ships. "We must give thanks," she said to the people.

"To our queen," they shouted. "Long live our queen."

And so, just as at Tilbury, Elizabeth knew that she had the heart of her people.

Elizabeth ruled England for 45 years, from 1558 to her death in 1603. The Elizabethan era was mostly a time of peace and stability for the nation. After the defeat of the Spanish Armada, England emerged as a commercial and naval power.

Elizabeth's reign is sometimes known as England's Golden Age because the arts flourished and great explorations of the world took place. It was a good time to be an actor. Playwrights William Shakespeare and Christopher Marlowe wrote and produced plays, some of which Elizabeth herself saw. English composers, such as William Byrd and Thomas Tallis, wrote music for the royal court. Poets, artists, and architects were also producing many new works. Meanwhile, British explorers traveled the seas. Sir Francis Drake was the first Englishman to circumnavigate the globe (1577–1580), and Sir Walter Raleigh, one of Elizabeth's favorites at court, established the first colony in North America.

STOP AND THINK

1. Why did Philip II send his armada to England?

2. Which leadership trait of Elizabeth's do you admire most? Why?

231

Ancient Artists

The cave paintings made by Paleolithic people show how important animals were to them. One cave in Lascaux, France, shows a few stick-figure people, no plants, and about 600 paintings of animals.

Paleolithic artists often used different-colored clays or earth for their paintings. They also used wood charcoal for black. Chalk, bone, or shell made white. Stones with mineral **veins** gave them red and yellow. The ancient artists didn't use such materials by accident. They figured out which materials made the best colors. They passed their "recipes" down through the generations.

LOOK IT UP

For more cave
paintings: Lascaux,
Ajanta, Altamira,
Chauvet-Pont-
d'Arc Cave

Kinds of Animals Shown in the Cave Art of Lascaux

Wild horses

Bison

Aurochs (a kind of ancient wild cattle)

Several kinds of deer

Several kinds of wild cats

Ibex (a kind of wild goat)

Mammoth (an extinct kind of elephant)

Bear

Rhinoceros

Fish

The Mystery of the Cave Art

The reason for the cave paintings is a mystery that archaeologists may never solve. They have some guesses. Maybe the pictures of animals were a way of telling about important hunts. Or perhaps the pictures were part of a religious ceremony, asking for successful hunts so the people could eat well.

The paintings do reveal something very important about Paleolithic people. They understood that they could use a **symbol** to stand for a real thing. They knew that a flat mark on a cave wall could show a living horse. This symbolic thinking was a huge leap forward for humankind. It was the beginning of art. It was also the beginning of using symbols to stand for ideas. One day this ability to make pictures would lead to written language.

STOP AND THINK

1. How can archaeologists tell what Paleolithic people ate?

2. Do you think art or fire was more important for early humans? Why?

233

TURNING POINT

Simón Bolívar and the Battle of Boyacá

FOCUS: How did Bolívar help Colombia win its independence?

Simon Bolivar and his followers

A single candle lit the mud hut where the army officers listened to their leader. Some men sat on the dirt floor; others sat on cattle skulls. Simón Bolívar was **outlining** a most daring plan. It was May 1819, and the 36-year-old Venezuelan dreamed of freeing all of South America from its Spanish colonial rulers. His immediate goal, though, was to liberate New Granada*.

RERED

Problem/Solution

What was Bolívar's goal? What problem made his goal seem impossible?

The fighting would be challenge enough, but the capital of New Granada lay high in the Andes mountains, on the other side of 13,000-foot peaks. How could this group of patriots get their troops and equipment across such **obstacles**? The journey appeared impossible, but Bolívar knew that it was the only route to his goal. And fortunately his officers believed in him.

*New Granada: present-day Colombia**

234

"Sir," said a colonel, "I, for one, will follow you even to Cape Horn!" (That is the continent's southern tip.)

Two days later, the patriot army set out in a pouring rain. The two thousand soldiers spent the next three weeks crossing the plains of Venezuela, on their way to the foothills of the Andes. With their cavalry horses and pack mules, they **forded** rivers and slogged through swamps, marching 20 miles a day. It was the rainy season, and soon everything was damp and rotting.

At the foot of the Andes, Bolívar was joined by his fellow patriot, General Francisco Santander, and about 1,000 soldiers. Together, the 3,000 men—along with their horses, mules, and cattle—began the ascent. As they dragged themselves up what seemed like **interminable** walls of rock, men began to die from cold and hardship. Most had never left the plains before; this was their first experience with cold weather and high **altitude**.

By the time the army got over the peaks and descended into a broad mountain valley, only 1,200 men and a few animals had survived. But the people of New Granada welcomed them as liberators, and Bolívar was able to secure food, medical care, new horses, and volunteers for his army.

As Bolívar had hoped, he took the Spanish army by surprise, for the colonial leaders were certain that no army could make it over the Andes. In a battle at the village of Tunja, Bolívar led his soldiers to victory. But the turning point came later, near a bridge over the Boyacá River, where Bolívar's army captured about 1,600 Spanish troops and their commander. Three days later, Simón Bolívar marched his soldiers into Bogotá, the capital of New Granada, whose people cheered him as "The Liberator."

Simón Bolívar was born in Venezuela in 1783. His family was wealthy, but because they were Creoles (of Spanish origin but born in South America) they could not hold positions in the government or military. Venezuela was a Spanish colony, and most important jobs were reserved for those born in Spain.

The biggest influence on Bolívar's early life was a tutor, Simón Rodríguez. Rodríguez taught Bolívar about democracy and equality. Bolívar told him, "You have molded my heart for liberty and justice, for the great and the beautiful."

REREAD

Problem/Solution

How does one group's solution become another group's problem?

STOP AND THINK

1. What were some of the challenges facing Bolívar and his men?

2. What kind of leader do you think Bolívar was?

ASSYRIAN EMPIRE

Euphrates R.

BABYLONIAN

Ni

Assur

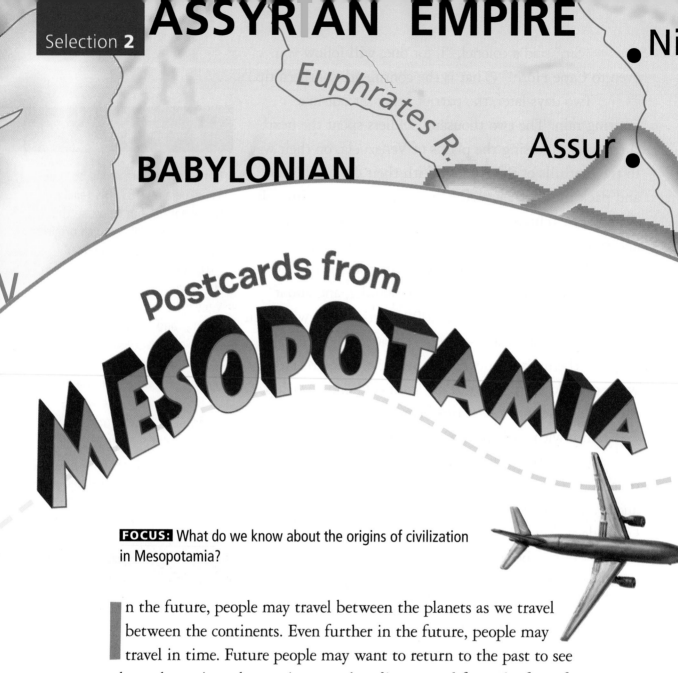

Postcards from

MESOPOTAMIA

FOCUS: What do we know about the origins of civilization in Mesopotamia?

In the future, people may travel between the planets as we travel between the continents. Even further in the future, people may travel in time. Future people may want to return to the past to see places that exist only as ruins—or that disappeared from the face of the earth long ago. Time travelers could go back thousands of years to see the Egyptian pyramids in all their glory. Roman Empire buffs could visit Rome during its heyday.

These high-definition plasmatronic postcards were sent by a time traveler far in the future. The traveler visited one of the first great civilizations, in Mesopotamia. This fertile area was located between the Tigris and Euphrates Rivers in what is now Iraq. She got a great package—she toured 8,000 years of history in one week.

Cuneiform Writing

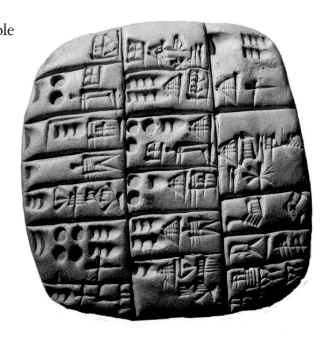

Dear Tanya,

The Mesopotamians have an incredible way of writing—they make marks in soft clay. Many of the symbols are pictures of the things they represent. A sheep, for example, has its own symbol, as does a bundle of grain, and a hand. In time, the symbol begins to stand for the sound of the word. These sounds are the beginnings of an alphabet. It all begins around 4000 B.C.E., but it will take another 2,000 years for this kind of writing to be widely used.

Love,
Grandma

237

The people must ask why. Why so many dead and what for? [*Lincoln sighs as he reads what appear to be notes.*]

This war has been a test, Lamon, a test of whether or not the Founders' vision—a nation based on equality—will endure. The dead who are to be reburied at Gettysburg have given their lives for the promise of this nation. We need a new call for freedom, my friend.

Scene 4 *November 19, 1863, the afternoon of a cool autumn day at Gettysburg, Pennsylvania, and President Lincoln sits in a reviewing stand at the new Soldiers' National Cemetery, surrounded by* **dignitaries**. *Ward Hill Lamon sits on his right. The Honorable Edward Everett is at the podium, concluding his long, oratorical speech.*

Everett: But they, I am sure, will join us in saying, as we bid farewell to the dust of these **martyr**-heroes, that wheresoever throughout the civilized world the accounts of this great warfare are read, and down to the latest period of recorded time, in the glorious annals of our common country, there will be no brighter page than that which relates the Battles of Gettysburg." [*Along with thunderous applause, the music of a military band can be heard in the background.*]

Scene 3 *A week later, President Lincoln and Ward Hill Lamon stand talking in a White House anteroom. Lamon, 19 years younger than Lincoln, is a good friend and former law partner of the president. Lincoln is dressed for outdoors, wearing his stovepipe hat. As they talk, Lincoln removes his hat and takes some crumpled papers from inside it.*

Lincoln [*waving the papers in Lamon's direction*]: Listen to this, Lamon. You know that I am to give a few words at the Gettysburg dedication. Thus I have made some notes, a memorandum of what I want to say, for I want to pronounce something worthy of the occasion.

Well, here is my thinking on the subject: our nation is torn asunder, thousands upon thousands of American men are dead, and many more will die.

Lamon [*speaking to Lincoln*]: Mr. Everett has spoken for almost two hours, but the crowd has certainly appreciated his words.

Lincoln: I have written just ten sentences, my friend, yet they say what I want to say about this war and this nation. [*He stands and walks to the podium. He begins speaking.*] Fourscore and seven years ago...

The Thirteenth Amendment to the U.S. Constitution was ratified in 1865.

Section 1. Neither slavery nor involuntary servitude, except as a punishment for crime whereof the party shall have been duly convicted, shall exist within the United States, or any place subject to their jurisdiction.

THE GETTYSBURG ADDRESS

Fourscore and seven years ago our fathers brought forth on this continent a new nation, conceived in liberty and dedicated to the proposition that all men are created equal.

Now we are **engaged** in a great civil war, testing whether that nation or any nation so conceived and so dedicated can long endure. We are met on a great battlefield of that war. We have come to dedicate a portion of that field as a final resting-place for those who here gave their lives that that nation might live. It is altogether fitting and proper that we should do this.

But, in a larger sense, we cannot dedicate, we cannot consecrate, we cannot hallow this ground. The brave men, living and dead, who struggled here have consecrated it far above our poor power to add or detract. The world will little note nor long remember what we say here, but it can never forget what they did here. It is for us the living rather to be dedicated here to the unfinished work which they who fought here have thus far so nobly advanced. It is rather for us to be here dedicated to the great task remaining before us—that from these honored dead we take increased devotion to that cause for which they gave the last full measure of devotion—that we here highly resolve that these dead shall not have died in vain, that this nation under God shall have a new birth of freedom, and that government of the people, by the people, for the people shall not perish from the earth.

STOP AND THINK

1. What was the occasion of Lincoln's Gettysburg speech?

2. How would you describe Lincoln's "ten sentences" at Gettysburg?

The Royal Cemetery at Ur

Dear Tanya,

I was fortunate to happen across the burial of a rich man at the royal cemetery. What a ceremony! What wealth! He must have had a musical background, for they buried him with several harps that were covered with precious stones, gold, silver, and bronze. Maybe he had a lot of wives, because they also buried a number of women's headdresses, each very ornate. The outsides of the tombs are equally **elaborate**.

Kisses,
Grandma

REREAD

Description

What does the description of the burial tell you about the dead man?

The First Written Laws and Stories

Dear Tanya,

The tribes who live in Mesopotamia are the first people to leave records of their laws—on cuneiform tablets. These laws tell who has to pay taxes. They also command that silver be paid to the poor. Some laws outlaw **corruption** in government. Others protect widows and orphans from rich men who might take advantage of them. Medical texts and religious works have been written down. And the epic story of my personal hero, Gilgamesh, is being recorded even now. Maybe I can find out which of our versions is the original.

Best,
Grandma

THE HANGING GARDENS OF BABYLON

The Hanging Gardens of Babylon and the Ishtar Gate

Dear Tanya,

This gorgeous ziggurat has royal gardens growing on the terraces of each level. Water is pumped from the Euphrates River for the gardens. According to the locals, King Nebuchadnezzar II built this amazing structure to make his wife happy. Her faraway homeland was unlike the hot, dry, brown plains of Mesopotamia. Later, the ancient Greeks will describe the ziggurat as a paradise of greenery. For me, it's certainly one of the seven wonders of the ancient world. The Ishtar Gate is massive, with beautiful **glazed** bricks in bright colors and horses in relief brickwork. These Babylonians really know how to decorate. See you soon.

Love,
Grandma

STOP AND THINK

1. How did Mesopotamians begin to write?

2. If you could travel back in time, where would you go?

241

MOHANDAS GANDHI was born in India in 1869, trained as a lawyer in England, and practiced law in South Africa—another country under British rule. One day in South Africa, Gandhi was asked by a white man to leave his first-class train carriage. When Gandhi refused, he was put off the train. Soon afterward he began to use nonviolent methods to work against the South African policies of racial discrimination. "I object to violence," he said, "because when it appears to do good, the good is only temporary; the evil it does is permanent."

Gandhi returned to India in 1914 to continue his work for justice and independence. He was already a widely respected spiritual leader. He had given up Western clothing and wore a simple homespun white cloth. He was a vegetarian, and followed the principles of *ahimsa* and *satyagraha*. *Ahimsa* and *satyagraha* are Hindu words that can be roughly translated as "nonviolence" and "devotion to the truth." Gandhi cared not only about the goal, but the means used to achieve it.

PD: On March 12, about 80 of Bapu's followers set out on a march from the **ashram** where we live. We marched 240 miles in 23 days. Bapu wanted people to understand what we were doing; therefore, all along the way, we stopped in villages to explain our objectives. And people joined us—so many people that eventually the line of marchers stretched for two miles. Look at these crowds here. There are thousands and thousands of people, Mr. Berger, which is a **testament** to our beloved leader.

....
ashram: the residence of a spiritual group and their leader

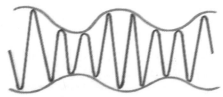

I must add that there have been reporters like you along the way— reporters from around the world. Bapu was quite pleased about this. "I want world sympathy in this battle of Right against Might," he said.

RNT: What happened when you arrived in Dandi, Mr. Desai?

PD: We arrived yesterday, as you know. First there were prayers, and then Bapu picked up a lump of mud filled with salt. "With this," he proclaimed, "I am shaking the foundations of the British Empire." He simply boiled the mud in seawater and made salt, thereby breaking the law. Then he asked everyone to make salt for themselves.

Mohandas Gandhi addressing followers

RNT: Mr. Desai, now I'd like to go back to something you mentioned earlier. Do you believe that Great Britain will give independence to India?

PD: In January of this year, Gandhi and the Indian National Congress issued our own Declaration of Independence. I have memorized some of its words: "We believe in the **inalienable** right of the Indian people, as of any other people, to have freedom.... We believe therefore, that India must sever the British connection and attain *Purna Swaraj,* or complete independence."

RNT: Thank you, Mr. Desai, thank you very much. I wish you good luck in your efforts. This is Mark Berger, signing off for Radio News Tonight.

FROM THE "QUIT INDIA SPEECH"
BY MAHATMA GANDHI, AUGUST 8TH, 1942

...Ours is not a drive for power, but purely a nonviolent fight for India's independence. In a violent struggle, a successful general has been often known to effect a military coup and to set up a dictatorship. But under the Congress scheme of things, essentially nonviolent as it is, there can be no room for dictatorship.... The Congress is unconcerned as to who will rule, when freedom is attained. The power, when it comes, will belong to the people of India....

STOP AND THINK

1. What was the goal of the Salt March?

2. Why do you think makes Gandhi's nonviolent methods successful?

The Phoenicians

MASTER SAILORS & TRADERS

FOCUS: Why did Phoenicia have such an influence in the Mediterranean region?

Phoenicia's reign over the eastern Mediterranean lasted only from 1200 to 800 B.C.E. Yet the country had an important **influence** on other societies. Phoenicians built the first ships with **keels**. A keel is a central timber that runs lengthwise in a ship's hull. Keels made it possible to build larger ships. So Phoenician trading ships could carry more materials than other trading ships. Phoenicia became a great trading nation. Its merchants took over the old Egyptian trade routes. And its navy went on to establish colonies in Africa, Sicily, Carthage, Sardinia, and Spain.

244

Shipbuilding

Phoenicians could sail on the open seas because their ships were well built. They used a new method to join pieces of wood. Pockets were cut into heavy timbers. A piece of wood was fitted into the pockets, joining two larger pieces. Finally, a peg was pounded into a hole drilled between the pieces. This construction held the ship together even in the worst storms.

Merchant Ships

The Phoenicians sailed across the Mediterranean Sea. They passed through the **Straits** of Gibraltar, then called the Pillars of Hercules. They journeyed to England to trade for tin. Some **accounts** claim that Phoenician merchants sailed around the Horn of Africa. Phoenician ships were about the same size as those that Columbus would use to cross the Atlantic—2,000 years later.

Trading Materials

Phoenician ships carried goods from port to port around the Mediterranean. Some of the most valuable goods were gold, glass, tin, cedar, and pine. One of Phoenicia's famous exports was fine linen, which was often dyed purple. (The dye was made from snail shells.) Returning merchants brought back papyrus, ivory, ebony, silk, amber, and many other goods.

Alphabet

The Phoenician alphabet used symbols to represent sounds. It was easier to read and write than cuneiform. This method of writing spread across the region and eventually developed into our alphabet.

STOP AND THINK

1. What made Phoenician ships better than other ships?

2. Which do you think is more important, trading goods or trading ideas?

THE BIG QUESTION:

HOW DO YOU KNOW WHEN YOU'VE DONE A GOOD JOB?

READINGS

10 MORE THAN WORDS

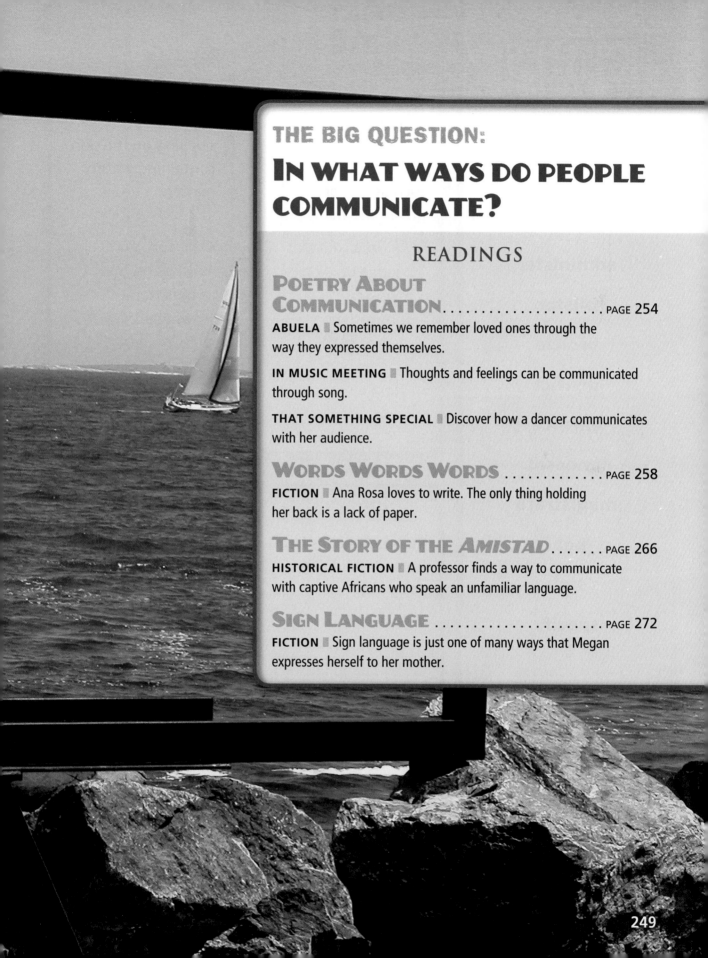

Literature Words

administer

Administer means to manage or be in charge of things such as law or government.

" In a court, a judge or magistrate administers justice. "

blister

A **blister** is a swelling on the skin containing watery matter.

" Tom got blisters on his hands from rowing all day. "

innocent

Innocent means free from wrongdoing; not guilty.

" The judge said the man was innocent and set him free. "

magistrate

A **magistrate** is a civil officer with the power to administer and enforce the law.

" The magistrate ordered the robber to go to jail. "

bronze

Bronze is a metal consisting of copper and tin.

66 A bronze statue was erected in the plaza. 99

district

A **district** is a region that is marked off for election or other government purposes.

66 Five hundred people from our district voted against the new hotel. 99

enforce

Enforce means to ensure that people obey rules and laws.

66 A police officer enforces the law. 99

peal

Peal refers to a loud, prolonged ringing of bells.

66 The bells pealed loudly when the victory was announced. 99

sigh

To **sigh** is to let out one's breath as from sorrow, weariness, or relief.

66 Jenna sighed when she broke her favorite cup. 99

specify

Specify means to mention or name specifically; to state in detail.

66 The owner specified the kind of worker he needed for the job. 99

Literature Words

amid

couple

crevice

curse

envy

frantic

serious

steady

tilted

utter

amid

Amid means surrounded by or in the middle of.

66 She found herself amid a crowd of people. 99

couple

A **couple** means two.

66 I only had a couple of dollars in my pocket. 99

frantic

Frantic means very emotional, fearful, or frustrated.

66 Ed was frantic when he couldn't find his homework. 99

serious

Serious means solemn, thoughtful, or deeply committed.

66 Lynn was serious about writing, and she wrote at least one page in her journal every day. 99

crevice

A **crevice** is a narrow crack or opening.

66 I lost the penny when it rolled into a crevice in the sidewalk. 99

curse

To **curse** is to use an expression of anger.

66 He was so angry he wanted to curse, but he remained silent. 99

envy

Envy is the desire to have what someone else has.

66 Mark's writing made him the envy of his classmates, who all wished they could write like him. 99

steady

Steady refers to things that happen in the same way again and again.

66 The waves broke on the shore in a steady motion, always with the same rhythm and pattern. 99

tilted

Tilted means slanted downward on one side.

66 He tilted the table and the ball rolled off the end. 99

utter

Utter means complete or total.

66 When the lights went out, there was utter darkness, and Jean couldn't read anymore. 99

Comprehension

✓ **TARGET SKILL** **Evidence** Writers do not always provide all the information readers need for a complete understanding of a story. For example, a writer may give general information about the setting but not specific information, such as the name of a town or state. When this is so, you can use your own knowledge from experience and evidence from the story to make inferences about specific details related to the story's setting. You can also make inferences about what the characters are like and how they feel. You can often find evidence by paying close attention to descriptive details and to what characters do and say.

Here is an excerpt from "Esperanza Learns New Jobs." You can infer several specific things about the main character and the setting from the evidence given here.

Esperanza is wearing old, ragged clothes, which she had to borrow from other people. This evidence reveals that she doesn't have money even for necessities.

This evidence reveals that the story is taking place in the winter. It is probably sometime in January, shortly after New Year's Day.

Esperanza bundled in all the clothing that she could put on, old wool pants, a sweater, a ragged jacket, a wool cap, and thick gloves over thin gloves, all borrowed from friends in the camp. . .

Since the driver could only see a few yards ahead, the truck rumbled slowly on the dirt roads. They passed miles of naked grapevines, stripped of their harvest and bereft of their leaves. Fading into the mist, the brown and twisted trunks looked frigid and lonely. . .

Esperanza's breath made smoky vapors in front of her face as she waited for the truck to take her to tie grapevines. She shifted from foot to foot and clapped her gloves hands together and wondered what was so new about the New Year. It already seemed old. . .

This evidence reveals that the action is taking place in a rural area, where not every road is paved.

You can use this graphic organizer to keep track of evidence from the story and inferences you make.

Clues	Inference
old wool pants, a sweater, a ragged jacket, a wool cap, and thick gloves over thin gloves	
all borrowed from friends in the camp	Esperanza cannot afford even necessary items.
the truck rumbled slowly on the dirt roads	The story is taking place in the countryside.
miles of naked grapevines	
stripped of their harvest and bereft of their leaves	
the brown and twisted trunks looked frigid and lonely	
Esperanza's breath made smoky vapors in front of her face.	
She shifted from foot to foot and clapped her gloves hands together and wondered what was so new about the New Year.	The action is taking place in the cold winter, probably sometime in January.

✓ **TARGET STRATEGY** **Infer** The author will often use details about the setting and the character's actions to help build toward the theme, or basic lesson, of the story. What do the clues about Esperanza's surroundings and actions help you infer about the theme of this selection?

Comprehension

✔ **TARGET SKILL** **Use Evidence** Writers do not always directly state everything you need for a complete understanding of a story. However, clues from the text, also called evidence, can help you make inferences about the characters and what they are doing. Pay close attention to what characters say and how they act. Use this evidence and your own knowledge from experience to make inferences. Doing so will give you a more complete understanding of a story.

Here is an excerpt from "Words, Words, Words." In it, the character Ana Rosa takes her brother's notebook so that she can write.

> **This is evidence that helps you understand that Ana Rosa is acting in a secretive way. She knows that she should not be using her brother's notebook.**

… I could write on a few pages and tear them out, I thought. Guario would never notice. I picked up a pencil and looked around. No one was coming.

So I wrote. First one page, then another and another … Suddenly the lights went out. It was another power blackout. A good thing, too, because I might not have stopped writing …

I tore out the pages carefully and slipped them into my pocket …

I felt the pages in my pocket. Just a couple more, I thought. No one would know at all. I tiptoed back inside and lit a candle. I sat at the table and wrote under the candle's light. I wrote one page after another until there were no more empty pages in Guario's notebook.

> **Have you ever been unable to stop doing something because you loved doing it? That experience and these details help you know that Ana Rosa simply cannot control her desire to write.**

You can use this graphic organizer to keep track of evidence from the story and inferences you make. Include your own thoughts and feelings under **Clues**.

Clues	Inferences
...I could write on a few pages and tear them out, I thought. →	
Guario would never notice. →	
I picked up a pencil and looked around. No one was coming. →	
I tore out the pages carefully and slipped them into my pocket... →	Ana Rosa hopes that no one will catch her. She knows that she should not be using her brother's notebook.
No one would know at all. →	
I've acted like this before. I know just how Ana Rosa is feeling. → →	
So I wrote. First one page, then another and another... →	
A good thing, too, because I might not have stopped writing... →	
Just a couple more, I thought. →	
I wrote one page after another until there were no more empty pages in Guario's notebook. →	Ana Rosa cannot control her desire to write.

✔ TARGET STRATEGY **Infer** You can use clues from a story and knowledge from your own experience to make inferences about the setting of a story, its characters, and how the characters feel about one another. As you read a story, pay close attention to the description of the setting and to details that describe what a character is doing.

WORDS WORDS WORDS

from

The Color of My Words

by Lynn Joseph

FOCUS: How can people express their most powerful dreams?

Ana Rosa lives with her parents, sister, and brother in a small seaside village in the Dominican Republic. No one in the community has much money, and life flows at a slow pace.

Ana Rosa loves to write, a fact that she has kept secret from everyone except her mother and her older brother, Guario. Her only notebook is the one she has for school, because her parents can't afford a notebook just for fun. So she writes on paper bags, napkins—any available scraps of paper. Ana Rosa envies Guario, because he has a notepad for his job as a waiter. She thinks about how wonderful it would be to have all those empty pages to fill with her writing. Then one day Guario forgets his notepad and leaves it out on a table.

Suddenly a breeze swirled through the house and flipped open the cover of Guario's notepad. The empty pages filled with wind and blew up one after the other, showing me all the lovely blank spaces waiting for words. I could write on a few pages and tear them out, I thought. Guario would never notice. I picked up a pencil and looked around. No one was coming.

So I wrote. First one page, then another and another. I stopped when I had filled five pages with words about Mount Isabel de Torres, and about Sosúa Beach, which I love. I wrote about the *niños*, and about climbing my favorite gri gri tree. I wrote a poem about Angela, my beautiful, silly older sister who knew nothing but how to smile at men passing by our porch. I wrote about my brother Roberto who worked hard in the sun renting beach chairs to tourists. Suddenly the lights went out. It was another power blackout. A good thing, too, because I might not have stopped writing.

I tore out the pages carefully and slipped them into my pocket. I went and sat on the porch and watched as the sky filled up its blue spaces with pinks and oranges and a deep, deep purple. **Utter** darkness swelled over everything. With the darkness was complete silence as well since the neighbors' radios could not blare out their loud *merengues*.

I felt the pages in my pocket. Just a **couple** more, I thought. No one would know at all. I tiptoed back inside and lit a candle. I sat at the table and wrote under the candle's light. I wrote one page after another until there were no more empty pages in Guario's notebook.

Feeling guilty about using up all the pages, Ana Rosa hides Guario's notepad under her mattress.

The next day, everybody in the house was looking for that notepad. Guario was shouting that he would be fired. That made Papi very frightened. Although Papi always swore that if he got up off his porch chair in the middle of the day, he'd get heatstroke, he, too, was helping to look for the book.

It was like a madhouse. Papi and Guario and Roberto and Angela and my little cousins were throwing everything out the front door in their **frantic** search. Chairs, a radio, old newspapers, clothes, shoes, our two dogs, some stray hens pecking at this and that, all went sailing into the dusty yard.

Of course, I knew exactly where it was—under my mattress—but I was too scared to say so. I pretended to help look around the house.

Ana Rosa goes nervously into the kitchen, where she finds her mother rolling out dough for empanadas. *Ana Rosa realizes that Mami knows who has taken the notepad, though Mami says nothing. Instead, Mami tells everyone sternly to come and eat, and to stop fussing about the notepad. The family gathers around the table. Mami has taken extra care with the meal, as though she is trying to distract everyone from being anxious about the notepad.*

We talked about where the notepad could be and what could have happened to it. Papi wasn't **cursing** anymore and Guario wasn't shouting.

Finally Papi reached into his pocket and took out some pesos. He put them on the table. Then Mami dug her hand deep into a pocket of her dress and put some pesos on the table, too. Roberto jumped up and went into the kitchen and came back with some pesos that he put next to Papi's and Mami's pesos. Guario looked surprised and I noticed that his eyes were turning bright red as if he were trying not to cry.

But that could not be possible. I had never seen Guario cry in my life. Guario was nineteen years old and he was my big, strong brother who took care of everything. Mami called him *Jefe* when Papi was not around. *Jefe* means "boss" and that is what Guario was. He worked two jobs and bought all our food and fixed everything that went wrong. He was always **serious**.

"Here," said Papi, pushing the pesos over to Guario, "take this and buy a new notepad for work."

Guario nodded and stood up. He walked around the table and kissed Mami on her cheek. Then he walked out the house to go to work.

I watched Guario's wide back move **steadily** away from us. When I turned around, Mami raised her eyebrows at me as if to say "What are you waiting for?"

I jumped up and ran after Guario. He was at the corner waiting for one of the noisy motorcycle taxis to take him to work.

"Guario," I called.

He turned around. I dashed up to him and threw my arms around his waist.

His hand smoothed down the flyaway hairs in my ponytail.

"I took your notepad," I whispered into his shirt. "I'm sorry."

Guario kept stroking my hair. After a while, he said, "I know what it feels like."

"How what feels like?" I asked.

"To want something so bad."

"What have you wanted so bad?" I asked, looking up at him.

"A future," he answered. And then I saw the tears in his eyes for real. This was not the first time I had heard Guario talk about wanting a future. I just never paid it any attention. But to be right there at that moment hearing and seeing him, the whole world tilted away from me, me, me to someone else—my big brother.

Guario and I stood at the corner with our arms around each other as all the motorcycle taxis drove by blowing their horns. It was the first time I knew that words could not tell everything.

STOP AND THINK

1. How do the other family members solve the problem of the missing notepad?

2. What can someone do when following his or her dream might hurt someone else?

Your Turn

Use Your Words:

absolute	gradual
attitude	huddled
awkward	indignation
blurt	pathetic
confinement	professor
discard	solitary
enslave	suggest
erect	taunt
focus	threshold
frustrate	vague

- Read the words on the list.
- Read the dialogue. Find the words.

My speech was the <u>absolute</u> worst. I <u>blurted</u> it out. It was <u>pathetic</u>.

Let me <u>suggest</u> something. First, stand <u>erect</u> and <u>focus</u> on the audience.

But <u>Professor</u> Lang, I feel so <u>awkward</u> up here.

MORE ACTIVITIES

1. Take a Survey
Graphic Organizer
Ask 12 classmates how they mostly communicate. Tally their answers. Share your findings with your class.

2. Make a Face
Speaking and Listening
People can communicate by making faces. With a partner, take turns making faces. The faces should communicate anger, happiness, sadness, and so on. See if your partner can guess what emotion or feeling you are expressing.

How Do You Communicate?

IM/Text Message	Write Notes	Cell Phone	E-mail	Talk Face-to-Face

3. Write a Poem
Writing

Think of a flower you like. For two minutes, write down as many words as you can that describe the flower. Rearrange the words to make a poem. It does not have to rhyme. Share your poem with your class.

4. Describing Yourself
Vocabulary and Writing

Think about yourself. List ten words that you would use to describe yourself.

5. Make a Speech
Speaking and Listening

Think of a topic you feel strongly about. Write a short speech about your topic. Work with a partner to refine your speech. When you are ready, give your speech to the class.

6. Share Ideas
Communication

How would you communicate if you and your partner didn't speak the same language? Without writing, speaking, or mouthing words, tell your partner to do something. Use only hand signals. See if your partner understands you.

The Story of the
AMISTAD

by Emma Gelders Sterne

FOCUS: How can you speak to someone whose language you don't know?

*I*n 1839, some Africans had been captured
and delivered across the Atlantic Ocean to the
Spanish colony of Cuba, where they were sold into
slavery. As the ship transporting the imprisoned
Africans sailed from one Cuban port to another,
the captives revolted. The Africans, who were not
experienced sailors, were unable to direct the ship,
the Amistad, home toward Africa, so it ended
up in the United States instead. Though many
Americans still favored slavery at that time, others
had a different **attitude**. They wanted to liberate
the Amistad Africans and prepared to take their
case to court. But how could the Africans, who
spoke a language nobody else understood, argue
their side of the story in front of a judge?

Some People You Need to Know

Cinque: the leader of the *Amistad* Africans

Marga, Ferni, Teme: female *Amistad* Africans

Ka-le: a young *Amistad* African

Ruiz and Montez: the Spanish owners of the *Amistad*

Josiah Gibbs: a **professor** of languages

Graham Ellis, Enoch Hopkins: people who want to free the Africans

Antonio: **enslaved** cabin boy on the *Amistad*; he can communicate with the Africans a little but has betrayed them

As this selection begins, the male captives have **huddled** in one locked room, while the young girls are being held in another. The Africans' leader, Cinque, has been chained elsewhere in **solitary confinement**. Two white men who oppose slavery, Graham Ellis and Enoch Hopkins, arrive at the New Haven building where the Africans are being imprisoned. Ellis and Hopkins have already met the African prisoners from the *Amistad*. Now, they are accompanied by Josiah Willard Gibbs, a language professor. Ellis and Hopkins are hoping that Professor Gibbs can communicate with an older African named Tua, who spoke words that resembled Arabic. However, Tua has recently died of an illness. When Ellis and the other white men notice that Tua and Cinque are missing, they ask the jailer, Mr. Pendleton, about them.

Slave holding pens

"Cinque?" the jailer showed surprise. "He's a dangerous murderer. I've got him downstairs in solitary. But I'll bring him up if you'll take the responsibility. I don't know about any sick man; this is all there is, in these two rooms. Except the little girls. My wife is fitting them with some decent dresses. I'll fetch 'em in, when she's clothed 'em proper."

The man unlocked a connecting door and disclosed another room full of captives. Then he went away, barring the door behind him.

While he waited, Graham Ellis moved from one silent group to another. Mr. Pendleton had said that none were missing except Cinque and some girls. Yet he did not find the sick man who had spoken words in Arabic.

The door opened once more, and Marga, Ferni, and Teme slipped in, robed from neck to ankle in stiff calico wrappers. They looked unhappy in the ugly garments. They did not leave the doorway.

No one spoke.

Outside the closed door the clanking of chains, the grating of a lock, the creaking of a door, sounded strangely loud in the silence. The door opened and Cinque stood **erect** on the **threshold**.

With cries of joy, the captives crowded around him. Cinque was still alive. He was with them again!

Cinque caught sight of Graham Ellis. Cinque moved toward him as to an old friend, hand upraised, eyes calm and confident.

Ka-le sighed in relief. He had been wrong to doubt these men and this boy. They came in friendship. He caught Enoch's eye and smiled.

Again Ellis spoke the names of Willard Gibbs and Enoch Hopkins. Then he spoke Tua's name, questioningly.

Cinque

At mention of Tua's name, there was a **vague** troubled stir in the room. The three girls, who had been hovering close to Cinque, slid down at his feet and dropped their heads.

"We wanted to see Tua," Ellis explained, "because he gave a greeting which sounded like *Salaam Aleikum*. These are words of a language Professor Gibbs can speak. Gibbs thought maybe he could talk with Tua, could help you."

As Ellis spoke, Cinque's eyes traveled to the anxious faces of his companions. He saw that they were frightened and sad at every mention of Tua's name. He knew then that Tua had died.

Professor Gibbs nudged Ellis. "I am afraid we are too late to speak to the man you seek. From the look on their faces, he is evidently no longer living."

"Must have died in New London then," the jailer said. "These you see were all that were handed over to my keeping. And a scared bunch they are, all but that one charged with murder."

"Professor Gibbs!" Enoch Hopkins said. "Isn't there any way to speak to them? You know so many languages!"

Willard Gibbs sighed. "Arabic seemed a real hope," he answered. "But I don't know a single African tongue, and if I did it wouldn't be likely to be the right one. Every tribe in Africa speaks its own language."

"But some of the Negroes in town—wouldn't some of them be able to speak?"

Slaves on board a ship

"The free Negroes in New Haven speak the language of the country they were born in, same as you and me," Gibbs answered. "Since the days of the Declaration of Independence there hasn't been an African slave brought to Connecticut. But you're right, that's what we've got to have—a native-born African of the same tribe as these people, and one who speaks English, too."

"However could we do that?" Ellis asked.

"If we had some clue to their language, we might look for seamen of their tribe on British ships. We could go down to the waterfront in Boston—or better still, New York. It's our only chance, and it'll take a miracle to turn up such a man."

Early diagram of a
slave ship

As the three white men whispered together, Cinque saw a
cloud cross the face of Graham Ellis. He guessed the problem—the
old problem of language. There was Antonio, of course. But after the
first thought, Cinque put that name from his mind. Once the
masters were in power, Antonio had shown his true colors, caring
little for the truth.

"What did you expect?" he had **taunted**, when the chains
were fastened to Cinque's wrists again. And to every lie Montez and
Ruiz had told the soldiers, the cabin boy had nodded in agreement.
Though Antonio spoke enough of the Mandingo tongue, he would
not be of use to them.

Ka-le was watching the white men, too. Suddenly he saw
Graham Ellis beckon him. The man called Gibbs held up a finger
and said a word in his own language. But Ka-le shook his head. He
could not understand.

Gibbs held up a second finger.

"What does he want to say?" Ka-le could have wept with
anxiety to understand.

A third finger was raised. Three fingers were held before his
face. Three words, one after the other, were spoken in the white
man's language.

270

Suddenly Ka-le had a thought. He too held up one finger. He spoke the word "one" in Mandingo. A second finger, followed by the word "two."

"By George!" Graham Ellis shouted. "The boy's got the notion! Write down the sounds, Professor Gibbs, I'll do the finger work, up to ten."

By this clever method, Professor Gibbs mastered the words for the numbers one through ten. He journeyed down to the docks in New York City to search for free African sailors who recognized and understood those ten words, until finally he located one who did—James Covey. Covey accompanied Gibbs back to Connecticut to act as an interpreter, allowing the imprisoned Africans to speak for themselves and give their own evidence in court. The *Amistad* captives had to appear at several hearings, including one in the U.S. Supreme Court. A former U.S. President, John Quincy Adams, acted as the Africans' defense lawyer before the Supreme Court. The verdict of the Supreme Court was that the imprisoned Africans deserved liberty and that they were entitled to depart for their native continent, Africa.

The Africans' case was first tried in this building.

STOP AND THINK

1. Why was it so important for Gibbs and his friends to be able to communicate with the Africans?

2. Why might you prefer to speak for yourself rather than having another person express your wishes or needs?

SIGN LANGU✋GE A

from *Leading Ladies* by MARLEE MATLIN and DOUG COONEY

FOCUS: What are some ways that people express themselves without words?

Some people speak with their voices and listen with their ears, while others "speak" with their hands and "listen" with their eyes. Sign language, which uses mostly hand and arm movements, is a language used by people who can't hear. Some deaf people can also use their voices and read lips, which helps them communicate with hearing people.

Because Megan is deaf but her mother, Lainee, can hear, both Megan and Lainee know how to sign and also how to speak. In this selection, Megan has had an embarrassing moment in school during a folk dance practice. When Megan and Lainee are together after school, Megan is able to use more than one way to express her ideas and feelings.

🖳 LOOK IT UP

For more on communication by the hearing impaired: telecommunications devices for the deaf, text telephone, closed captioning, American Sign Language

M egan and her mother, Lainee, had their own form of sign language. When Megan got home from school that day, she wanted to tell her mother about that **awkward** moment after the polka—when all the kids had laughed and she felt a little lonely, different, and weird.

Instead of searching for the words in sign language, Megan sat on a kitchen stool and slumped across the counter. Her arm sprawled so that her knuckles knocked into the bread box. Her face pressed against the tiles so that one cheek smooshed and her lips puckered. Her legs dangled off the stool like a **discarded** rag doll, and her weight rocked the stool on its legs as though it might tumble to the ground at any moment. Her whole body turned into a **pathetic** little sigh.

It worked. Lainee turned from the sink, took one look at Megan—and said, "Okay—what?"

Megan shrugged and let her **focus** wander in another direction—which was her sign for "I don't want to talk about it but keep asking me questions."

Lainee reached for a bunch of white grapes, ran them under a quick blast of water in the sink, bundled them in a paper towel, and dropped them on the counter. She dragged a kitchen stool opposite Megan and pulled her daughter upright so that they were sitting knee-to-knee.

"Something's going on," said Lainee. "Tell me what it is."

Megan tugged a grape from the bunch and popped it into her mouth. She looked directly at her mother and let her eyes go blank—and then she began to chew.

"Is it school?" asked Lainee.

Megan scratched her cheek.

"Kids at school?" asked Lainee.

Megan shrugged. She plucked another grape, bit it in two, and studied the half that remained between her fingers.

"You're lonely, maybe? Misunderstood?" said Lainee.

Megan didn't want to say yes too quickly, but she did want to let her mother know that she was warm. She sat up on the stool, let the grape wander to the opposite cheek—and continued to chew.

"Did somebody say something to upset you?"

Megan stopped chewing—which was a sign for "yes."

"Do you want to tell me what they said?"

Megan started chewing again—which was a sign for "no."

REREAD

Inference

How does Megan's behavior show her mood?

"Megan, honey," said her mother, smacking the counter in **frustration**, "I'm not playing Twenty Questions! Please stop sulking and just tell me what's wrong! You know I love you, but it drives me crazy when you won't speak your mind!"

274

Megan didn't hold it in a moment longer. "Kids laughed at me!" she **blurted**—both in sign and speech.

Her mother was quiet, but only for a moment. "Oh, I see," she said. She reached for a grape to pop into her mouth. "And were you being silly?"

"No!" Megan erupted with **indignation**. "Mom! I was being **absolutely** serious and everybody laughed at me!"

"Well, you can be silly sometimes, so it wasn't a completely stupid question," her mother replied evenly. "Do you want to tell me what happened?"

Megan fingered a grape but didn't tug it from the bunch. "We were learning the polka," she said, "and Ms. Endee said we should do the polka for the whole school—but I was the only one who wanted to dance. Somebody said I should do a 'solo'—which means doing the polka all by myself, which is stupid because you dance the polka with a partner—but anyway I said, 'What's wrong with that? What's wrong with a solo? Why can't I dance all by myself?' And that's when everybody laughed at me."

Lainee let a moment pass before she spoke. Even then, all she said was, "Aw, honey."

"You think it's funny, too," said Megan.

"Am I laughing?" her mother replied. "You know I would never laugh at you. I would love to see you dance a solo. Polka or otherwise. Anytime!"

"So why were they laughing?" asked Megan.

"Maybe it was fun to imagine you dancing all by yourself," her mom replied. "Maybe they were laughing because they were delighted."

Megan looked down her nose at her mother. "You don't seriously believe that," she said.

275

"Maybe," her mom continued. "I don't know; I wasn't there! All I know is that you can't worry about what other people think. You'll drive yourself crazy that way. What you need to do is to be like the army!"

"Be like the army?" asked Megan.

"Be all that you can be!" said Lainee. "All you can do is to be you."

"But I'm already me," said Megan. "Who else could I be?"

"I meant like—be the best you can be," said her mother.

"They were laughing because I'm deaf," said Megan.

"I don't think that's true," her mother said quickly.

"Then because I'm different," Megan argued.

"We're all different," said her mother, giving up on the grapes.

"Not different like me," said Megan.

"You know what I think?" her mother **suggested**. "I think you should get on the computer and have a good talk with Lizzie, your friend from summer camp."

Megan smiled. She always smiled at the thought of Lizzie, this great girl that she and Cindy had met at summer camp. Lizzie also happened to be deaf but she didn't have the ability to speak, as Megan did. Lizzie spoke only sign language but they both read lips.

Not surprisingly, Megan and Lizzie became fast friends—which made Megan's best friend Cindy uncomfortable at first, but now they all got along. Unfortunately, Lizzie lived in Long Grove, a suburb on the absolute other side of the city than the suburb where Megan lived, almost an hour away. Lizzie attended the Illinois School for the Deaf, an all-deaf school, so she and Megan almost never had a chance to get together. Even so, they spoke often enough using the video phone.

Megan was always happy to hop on the video phone, but she still didn't understand how that was going to help her problem. "Why call Lizzie?" she asked her mom. "Lizzie wasn't at my school today. She doesn't know what happened. What is Lizzie going to tell me?"

"It always makes you happy when you talk to Lizzie," her mother urged. "And I hate to see you feeling so down." She ran her hand across Megan's face and gently stroked her hair. "Besides," she continued, "I bet Lizzie has been blue a few times, too. I bet she's had a few days when she was tired of seeming different and felt out there all by herself. If you talk to Lizzie, maybe you won't feel quite so 'solo.' "

Megan didn't respond, but she smiled a little bit. **Gradually** she straightened up on the kitchen stool. She hadn't even spoken with Lizzie yet—but she already felt better.

"Hit the computer," said Lainee, slapping her daughter's knee. "I have to get supper ready." As Lainee moved toward the refrigerator, Megan hopped off the stool and headed for the alcove where they kept the family computer.

When Megan activates the computer, she connects with Lizzie by video screen, allowing the two deaf friends to communicate by sign language, though they are miles apart. Later on, Megan is able to find a new way to express herself at school—she tries out for a play. Acting on stage is another way for people to raise their voices loud and clear.

STOP AND THINK

1. What are the different ways in which Megan communicates with her mother and with Lizzie?

2. With whom in your life can you communicate without words?

GLOSSARY

A

absolute (ăb′sə lo̅o̅t) – complete and certain; free from any limitations or restrictions

account (ə kount′) – an oral or written description or report of events

accuse (ə kyo̅o̅z′) – to charge with a wrongdoing; to blame

amid (ə mĭd′) – in the middle of or surrounded by

angle (ăng′gəl) – the figure or space formed by the coming together in a point of two lines or surfaces

appoint (ə point′) – to choose or assign by authority; to place in an office or job

architect (är′kĭ tĕkt) – a person who designs buildings

argue (är′gyo̅o̅) – to persuade by giving reasons for or against something

artifact (är′tə făkt) – any object made or shaped by people, especially things of archaeological or historical interest

assault (ə sôlt′) – violent or overwhelming attack or onslaught

atmosphere (ăt′mə sfîr) – the mixture of gases surrounding Earth, the stars, or other planets

attest (ə tĕst′) – to provide clear proof of, or to declare to be true or genuine

attitude (ăt′ĭ to̅o̅d) – manner, state of mind, or position towards someone or something

B

avalanche (ăv′ə lănch) – a large mass of snow or rock that tumbles down a mountainside; a massive or overwhelming amount of something

awkward (ôk′wərd) – difficult or uncomfortable to manage; embarrassing

barge (bärj) – a large, flatbottomed boat for carrying goods, usually pushed or towed by another boat

bear (bâr) – to carry or support something

bellow (bĕl′ō) – to shout loudly and powerfully

bewilder (bĭ wĭl′dər) – to puzzle or confuse

biologist (bī ŏl′ə jəst) – a person who studies living things

blacksmith (blăk′smĭth) – a person who makes and fits horseshoes, or shapes iron with an anvil and hammer

blurt (blûrt) – to voice something suddenly and impulsively

botanist (bŏt′n ĭst) – a person who studies plants

bounty (boun′tē) – giving liberally; generosity; a generous gift

brief (brēf) – short in length; lasting only a short time

bristle (brĭs′əl) – a short, stiff hair

brochure (brō sho̅o̅r′) – a small booklet or pamphlet containing information

C

canal (kə năl′) – an artificial waterway cut through land and used for irrigation or navigation

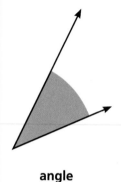

angle

bear

ă pat / ā pay / âr care / ä father / ĕ pet / ē bee / ĭ pit / ī pie / îr pier /
ŏ pot / ō toe / ô paw / oi noise / o̅o̅ took / o̅o̅ boot / ou out / ŭ cut /

capital (kăp′ĭ tl) – the city that is the official seat of government in a country or state

cease (sēs) – to put an end to, or to come to an end; to stop

character (kăr′ək tər) – a person, especially a noticeable or memorable one

clench (klĕnch) – to close tightly, as with teeth or fingers

cling (klĭng) – to remain in close contact with or stick to something

cloak (klōk) – a loose, sleeveless outer garment such as a cape

collide (kə līd′) – to come together with a violent, direct impact

colony (kŏl′ə nē) – a settlement of people from another country or nation who have moved to a new land, but are still controlled by their mother country

company (kŭm′pə nē) – a business or firm

comply (kəm plī′) – to do as one is asked or ordered

comrade (kŏm′răd) – a friend or companion who shares one's activities

concept (kŏn′sĕpt) – a general idea or mental image of something

confinement (kən fīn′mənt) – being shut up or kept within certain strict limits

conform (kən fôrm′) – to keep with or go along with the standards or general customs

conquest (kŏn′kwĕst) – winning or overcoming something by effort, as by war; a victory

corrupt (kə rŭpt′) – guilty of dishonest and immoral practices, such as bribery

couple (kŭp′əl) – a pair; two of a kind

crater (krā′tər) – a bowl-shaped cavity or dent

crescent (krĕs′ənt) – a narrow, curved shape that comes to a point at each end

crevice (krĕv′ĭs) – a narrow opening or crack, such as those found between rocks

crude (krōōd) – rough; not well finished

cultivate (kŭl′tə vāt) – to prepare and use land for crops; to grow and tend crops

curse (kûrs) – an expression of anger, sometimes using swearwords

cycle (sī′kəl) – a series of events that repeat regularly in the same order

cylinder (sĭl′ən dər) – an object or shape with straight sides and round ends, such as a can

D

dainty (dān′tē) – small, pretty, and delicate

dare (dâr) – to have the courage to take the risk of or face

data (dā′tə) – organized facts or information used for discussing or deciding something

debris (də brē′) – scattered broken pieces of something, like wreckage or litter

definite (dĕf′ə nĭt) – clear, unmistakable; with exact limits

defy (dĭ fī′) – to resist, withstand, or be unaffected by

demand (dĭ mănd′) – a desire for goods and services combined with the ability to purchase them

demonstrate (dĕm′ən strāt) – to show clearly and deliberately, especially by examples or actions

cloak

debris

dike

embroider

desire (dĭ zīr′) – a wish or longing for

device (dĭ vīs′) – an invention or thing that is made or used for a particular purpose

dike (dīk) – a bank of earth for controlling the waters of the sea or a river

direction (dĭ rĕk′shən) – the line along which anything moves or faces

discard (dĭ skärd′) – to throw away as useless or unwanted

distribute (dĭ strĭb′yo͞ot) – to pass out, to spread or scatter

diverse (dĭ vûrs′) – differing; unlike one another

domesticate (də mĕs′tĭ kāt′) – to train animals or plants to live in a human environment and be of use to humans

dramatic (drə mǎt′ĭk) – powerful, impressive, exciting; relating to a play in the theater

dreadful (drĕd′fəl) – terrible; fearsome; shocking

drift (drĭft) – to be carried by a current of water or air, or to move as if carried along by a current

dud (dŭd) – something that fails to work or is ineffective

E

edible (ĕd′ə bəl) – fit to be eaten; food

elaborate (ĭ lǎb′ər ĭt) – with many parts or details; complicated

electronic (ĭ lĕk trŏn′ĭk) – operated by a flow of electrons in a vacuum, gas, or certain solids

element (ĕl′ə mənt) – one of the parts or components that make up a whole

ember (ĕm′bər) – small piece of glowing ash or wood remaining from a fire

embroider (ĕm broi′dər) – to decorate by using needle and thread to sew a design onto fabric

empire (ĕm′pīr) – a group of nations or territories ruled by a single supreme power

employ (ĕm ploi′) – to put to use or put to work

enslave (ĕn slāv′) – to make into a slave

envy (ĕn′vē) – a feeling of discontent arising from wanting the qualities or possessions of another

epidemic (ĕp′ ĭ dĕm′ĭk) – a rapid spread, growth, or development, as with a disease

erect (ĭ rĕkt′) – standing upright or vertical

erode (ĭ rōd′) – to wear away gradually, as earth by wind or water

escape (ĭ skāp′) – get free of or get away from something

establish (ĭ stăb′lĭsh) – to set up on a permanent basis; to settle securely in place

exhaust (ĭg zôst′) – to use up or wear out completely; to tire out

expedition (ĕk′spĭ dĭsh′ən) – a journey or voyage for a particular purpose; the people making such a journey

F

fascinate (făs′ə nāt) – to attract and hold the interest of someone or something

feature (fē′chər) – a distinctive or noticeable characteristic of something

fertile (fûr′tl) – rich in the materials needed to support plant life; able to produce abundant plant life

ă pat / ā pay / âr care / ä father / ĕ pet / ē bee / ĭ pit / ī pie / îr pier /
ŏ pot / ō toe / ô paw / oi noise / o͝o took / o͞o boot / ou out / ŭ cut /

fleet (flēt) – a number of ships, aircraft, or vehicles under one command

fling (flĭng) – to throw with violence

focus (fō′kəs) – to give close attention to or concentrate on

frantic (frăn′tĭk) – wildly excited by fear, pain, passion, or anxiety

frolic (frŏl′ĭk) – to play about in a lively, cheerful way

frustrate (frŭs′trāt) – to cause feelings of discouragement or disappointment

furious (fyŏŏr′ē əs) – showing extreme anger; raging

G

generation (jĕn′ə rā′shən) – members of a family at a single stage in the descent of that family, or people born about the same time

geologist (jē ŏl′ə jəst) – a person who studies Earth's crust

gesture (jĕs′chər) – an expressive movement or action to show one's attitude or intentions

glacier (glā′shər) – a huge mass of ice moving slowly over land

glazed (glāzd) – coated with glass or another glossy surface

gradual (grăj′ōō əl) – taking place slowly or by degrees; little by little

grain (grān) – a small, hard particle, such as a seed or a crystal in a rock

gravity (grăv′ĭ tē) – the force that attracts bodies toward a larger body in space

graze (grāz) – to eat growing grass or other vegetation

grit (grĭt) – tiny, rough grains of stone or sand

H

harsh (härsh) – rough and disagreeable; severe; cruel

hollow (hŏl′ō) – empty or having a space inside; not solid

huddle (hŭd′l) – to crowd closely together in a small space

hunch (hŭnch) – a feeling or suspicion about something

I

ideal (ī dē′əl, ī dēl′) – regarded as perfect or as a standard of excellence

igneous (ĭg′nē əs) – formed by volcanic action

ill (ĭl) – physically or mentally unwell; unhealthy

imagination (ĭ măj′ə nā′shən) – the ability to form mental images

immigrate (ĭm′ĭ grāt) – to come into and settle in a country

impress (ĭm prĕs′) – to affect someone strongly, often favorably

indignation (ĭn′dĭg nā′shən) – strong displeasure at something felt to be unfair, mean, or unworthy

inflation (ĭn flā′shən) – a general increase in price of consumer goods, or a decrease in the purchasing power of money

influence (ĭn′flōō əns) – the power to affect a person, thing, or course of events

insolent (ĭn′sə lənt) – rude, insulting, or disrespectful

interest (ĭn′trĭst) – a sum earned for the use of money placed in a bank, or charged for borrowing money; usually a percentage of the amount used or borrowed

invest (ĭn vĕst′) – to use or spend money in order to gain a financial return or profit

glacier

igneous rock

ûr firm / hw which / th thin / *th* this / zh vision /
ə about, item, edible, gallop, circus

irrigation (ĭr′ĭ gāt′shən) – a supply of water for land by means of ditches, pipes, or streams

issue (ĭsh′ōō) – to give out, distribute, or publish something

K

keel (kēl) – the main structure, running lengthwise along the base of a ship, to which the ship's framework is attached

keel

L

launch (lônch) – to send something on its way by hurling or thrusting

lunar (lōō′nər) – relating to or referring to the moon

M

magnify (măg′nə fī) – to make something appear larger than it really is

makeshift (māk′shĭft) – a temporary or improvised substitute

margin (mär′jĭn) – the blank edge or border around printed matter on a page

mayor (mā′ər) – the head of a town or city

medium (mē′dē əm) – a substance or environment in which something grows or exists

metamorphic (mĕt′ə môr′fĭk) – rock changed in form or structure by extreme pressure or heat

misfortune (mĭs fôr′chən) – bad luck; an unlucky or undesirable event

mission (mĭsh′ən) – an assigned or self-imposed duty or task

monitor (mŏn′ĭ tər) – to check on or record; to test a process, system, or thing

orchard

monument (mŏn′yə mənt) – an impressive structure, such as a building or sculpture, built as a memorial

muddle (mŭd′l) – a disordered condition; a mess

N

nestle (nĕs′əl) – to snuggle comfortably in a sheltered position

nobles (nō′bəlz) – those belonging to the upper class of a country by birth or rank

noted (nō′tĭd) – famous, well known, or respected

nuclear (nōō′klē ər) – of, or using the energy that is released during reactions taking place in the center, or nucleus, of atoms

O

obsidian (ŏb sĭd′ē ən) – a smooth volcanic glass, usually black, often with sharp edges

occasional (ə kā′zhə nəl) – happening from time to time, but not regularly or frequently

odds (ŏdz) – the chance that a certain thing will happen compared to the chance that it will not happen

orbit (ôr′bĭt) – to travel in a curved path around a larger body in space

orchard (ôr′chərd) – a piece of land planted with fruit or nut trees

order (ôr′dər) – the way in which things happen or are placed in relation to one another

P

panic (păn′ĭk) – a sudden, overpowering terror or fear

passage (păs′ĭj) – a movement from one place to another by going by, over, through, or across; the path taken for that movement

ă pat / ā pay / âr care / ä father / ĕ pet / ē bee / ĭ pit / ī pie / îr pier /
ŏ pot / ō toe / ô paw / oi noise / ŏŏ took / ōō boot / ou out / ŭ cut /

patch (păch) – an area on a surface that is different in appearance from the rest of the surface

pathetic (pə thĕt′ĭk) – arousing pity or sadness

patient (pā′shənt) – able to face difficulty and troubles calmly; capable of waiting calmly

pebble (pĕb′əl) – a small stone worn smooth by the action of water

persecute (pûr′sĭ kyo͞ot) – to treat others cruelly or meanly, especially if they are of a different race or religion

phase (fāz) – a stage of change or a development in a cycle, such as a phase of the moon

planet (plăn′ĭt) – one of the large bodies in space that moves around a star

plateau (plă tō′) – an area of fairly level high ground

plunge (plŭnj) – to thrust forcefully into something

potential (pə tĕn′shəl) – capable of being but not yet in existence; a possibility

pouch (pouch) – a small bag often closing with a drawstring

powerful (pou′ər fəl) – having great strength, energy, or influence

praise (prāz) – to express approval or admiration of

preserve (prĭ zûrv′) – to protect and keep in unchanged condition for future use or enjoyment

product (prŏd′əkt) – something that is created or manufactured

production (prə dŭk′shən) – the process of creating or manufacturing something

professor (prə fĕs′ər) – a college or university teacher of the highest rank

profit (prŏf′ĭt) – the return or gain from an investment or action

province (prŏv′ĭns) – a territory or part of a country governed as a unit

provisions (prə vĭzh′ənz) – a stock of necessary supplies, especially food and drink

psychology (sī kŏl′ə jē) – a sly tactic or argument used to influence another

Q

quarry (kwôr′ē) – an open pit from which stone is obtained

R

rate (rāt) – a measure of a part, such as a percentage, of a whole

ration (răsh′ən) – a fixed amount allowed each person, especially of food; or to allow only a certain amount

recent (rē′sənt) – happening in a time shortly before the present

reflect (rĭ flĕkt′) – to throw back light, heat, or sound, or to give back an image, like a mirror

regret (rĭ grĕt′) – to feel sorry or disappointed or distressed about

reign (rān) – a period of royal rule or rule by a dominating power

relate (rĭ lāt′) – to have a connection with

remains (rĭ mānz′) – ancient ruins, fossils, or other objects that have survived from earlier times

reptile (rĕp′tīl) – a member of a group of cold-blooded animals that have a backbone, breathe through lungs, and are covered with scales or plates

resemble (rĭ zĕm′bəl) – to be like or similar to

reservoir (rĕz′ər vwär) – a natural or man-made pond or lake used for storing water

plateau

reptile

ûr firm / hw which / th thin / *th* this / zh vision /
ə about, item, edible, gallop, circus

sedimentary rock

sludge

resist (rǐ zǐst′) – to try to keep something from happening or from being successful

reverse (rǐ vûrs′) – opposite order or direction

revolve (rǐ vǒlv′) – to turn around or to rotate in a circular orbit

ritual (rǐch′ōō əl) – the series or order of actions used in a ceremony

s

salary (săl′ə rē) – a fixed payment for work done, given out on a regular basis

scaly (skā′lē) – covered with thin, overlapping plates that protect the skin of many fish and reptiles

screech (skrēch) – a harsh, high-pitched scream or sound

scurry (skûr′ē) – to move quickly or hurry along

sedimentary (sěd′ə měn′tə rē) – formed from sand, gravel, or silt carried by water

separate (sěp′ə rāt) – to divide or keep apart

serious (sîr′ē əs) – solemn and thoughtful; not smiling

shingle (shǐng′gəl) – a thin, rectangular piece of material such as wood, used in overlapping rows to cover a roof or the sides of a building

shortage (shôr′tǐj) – a lack of something that is needed

silt (sǐlt) – very fine particles of soil deposited by water

site (sīt) – the place where an activity takes place (or took place), or where a town or building stands (or stood)

situation (sǐch′ōō ā′shən) – a place or circumstance that something is in

sludge (slǔj) – a thick, muddy, oozing substance

smother (smǔth′ər) – to cover thickly or suffocate

soar (sôr) – to rise very high, as in flight

sober (sō′bər) – serious and self-controlled; straightforward

solemn (sǒl′əm) – serious, not smiling and cheerful

solitary (sǒl′ǐ těr′ē) – alone, without companions

sphere (sfîr) – something that has a perfectly round shape, such as a ball or a planet

stable (stā′bəl) – not changed or moved easily

steady (stěd′ē) – free, or almost free, from change or variation; happening in an even and regular manner, without variation

strain (strān) – to make excessive demands upon, or stretch to the limit

strait (strāt) – a narrow stretch of water connecting two larger bodies of water

strategy (străt′ə jē) – a plan of action for achieving something

striking (strī′kǐng) – very noticeable or impressive

strive (strīv) – to make a great effort

structure (strǔk′chər) – something that is built or constructed, such as a building or a bridge

struggle (strǔg′əl) – to work very hard; to make a great effort

style (stīl) – the way in which something is said, written, expressed, or done

stylish (stī′lǐsh) – fashionable and up-to-date

succeed (sək sēd′) – to accomplish something desired or intended

---

ă pat / ā pay / âr care / ä father / ě pet / ē bee / ǐ pit / ī pie / îr pier /
ǒ pot / ō toe / ô paw / oi noise / ŏŏ took / ōō boot / ou out / ǔ cut /

suggest (səg **jĕst′**) – to propose an idea or plan

suit (so͞ot) – to be appropriate for, fit, or meet the requirements for

summit (sŭm′ĭt) – the highest point or level that can be reached

suppose (sə **pōz′**) – to consider as a suggestion; to imagine

supreme (so͞o **prēm′**) – the most outstanding or highest in importance or quality

surface (sûr′fəs) – the outside of an object, or the top of an object such as a desk, or the top of a body of water or liquid

suspend (sə **spĕnd′**) – to hang or to keep from falling or sinking

swivel (swĭv′əl) – a link that allows the free turning of attached parts

symbol (sĭm′bəl) – something that is used for, or regarded as, representing something else

system (sĭs′təm) – a set of connected things or parts that form a whole or work together

T

task (tăsk) – a piece of work or job to be done

taunt (tônt) – to mock, insult, ridicule, or jeer at

threshold (thrĕsh′ōld) – the wood or stone forming the bottom of a doorway

tilted (tĭlt′ əd) – in a sloping or inclined position

tiresome (tīr′səm) – annoying, or causing tiredness or boredom

trample (trăm′pəl) – to walk or tread heavily or destructively

transfix (trăns fĭks′) – to make someone motionless with fear or amazement

U

universe (yo͞o′nə vûrs) – all existing things, including Earth, the galaxies, and everything else in space

urban (ûr′bən) – located in or related to a city or a town

utter (ŭt′ər) – complete or absolute

V

vague (vāg) – not clearly felt

vary (vâr′ē) – to be of different kinds; to change

vein (vān) – a narrow strip of a different color or material in substances such as rock, wood, or cheese

volunteer (vŏl ən tîr′) – a person who does something or offers to do something of his or her own free will

W

wane (wān) – to slowly decrease in size, brightness, or strength

wax (wăks) – to slowly increase in size, brightness, or strength

wealthy (wĕl′thē) – rich; having many valuables

weary (wîr′ē) – very tired mentally or physically

whine (hwīn) – to make a long, high, complaining sound, like that of a child or a dog

whirlpool (hwûrl′po͞ol) – a current of water that turns in a circle, sometimes pulling things to its center

wisdom (wĭz′dəm) – understanding what is true or right; good judgment

wit (wĭt) – the natural ability to understand; intelligence

witness (wĭt′nĭs) – to see or hear something, or a person who sees or hears something

urban

whirlpool

Acknowledgments

"Until I Saw the Sea" by Lillian Moore. Copyright © 1967 by Lillian Moore. Reprinted by permission of Random House, Inc.

"Sea Shell" from *The Complete Poetical Works of Amy Lowell*. Copyright © 1955 by Houghton Mifflin Company, renewed 1983 by Houghton Mifflin Company, Brinton P. Roberts, and D'Andelot Belin Esq. Reprinted by permission of Houghton Mifflin Harcourt Publishing Company. All rights reserved.

"The Crow and the Water Jug" by Eve Rice from *Once in a Wood: Ten Tales from Aesop* adapted by Eve Rice. Copyright © 1979 by Eve Rice. Reprinted by permission of Greenwillow Books, a division of HarperCollins Children's Books.

"Keys to the Universe" from *The Bellybutton of the Moon and Other Summer Poems* by Francisco X. Alarcón. Poems copyright © 1998 by Francisco X. Alarcón. Illustrations copyright © 1998 by Maya Christina Gonzales. Reprinted by permission of Children's Book Press, San Francisco, CA, www.childrensbookpress.org.

"March" by Elizabeth Coatsworth from *Summer Green* by Elizabeth Coatsworth. Copyright © 1948 by Macmillan Publishing Company; copyright renewed ©1976 by Elizabeth Coatsworth Beston. Reprinted by permission of Simon & Schuster Books for Young Readers, an imprint of Simon & Schuster Children's Publishing Division.

"Magnifying Glass" from *All the Small Poems* by Valerie Worth. Poems copyright © 1987 by Valerie Worth. Reprinted by permission of Farrar, Straus & Giroux LLC.

"These Shoes of Mine" by Gary Soto from *You're On! Seven Plays in English and Spanish* selected by Lori Marie Carlson. Reprinted by permission of HarperCollins Children's Books, a division of HarperCollins Publishers, Inc.

"The Project Starts Small" from *Project Mulberry* by Linda Sue Park. Text copyright © 2005 by Linda Sue Park. Reprinted by permission of Houghton Mifflin Harcourt Publishing Company.

"The Moon's the North Wind's Cooky" by Vachel Lindsay. Copyright © 1963, 1964 by Macmillan Company Inc. Reprinted by permission of Simon & Schuster Children's Publishing, a division of Simon & Schuster Inc.

"Full Moon" from *Sing to the Sun* by Ashley Bryan. Copyright © 1992 by Ashley Bryan. Reprinted by permission of HarperCollins Children's Books, a division of HarperCollins Publishers, Inc.

"In the Orchard" by James Stephens from *Magic Verse*, edited by Charles Causley. Copyright © 1915 by the Macmillan Company, renewed 1943 by James Stephens. *Magic Verse* copyright © 1974 by Charles Causley. Reprinted by permission of Simon & Schuster Children's Publishing, a division of Simon & Schuster, Inc.

"Another Mountain" by Abiodun Oyewole. Copyright © 1983 by Abiodun Oyewole. Reprinted by permission of the author.

The Color of My Words by Lynn Joseph. Copyright © 2000 by Lynn Joseph. All rights reserved. Reprinted by permission of HarperCollins Children's Books, a division of HarperCollins Publishers, Inc.

The Ear, the Eye, and the Arm by Nancy Farmer. Copyright © 1991 by Nancy Farmer. Reprinted by permission of Orchard Books, an imprint of Scholastic Inc.

"The Wind" from *Complete Poems for Children* (Heinemann) by James Reeves. Copyright © by James Reeves. Reprinted by permission of the James Reeves Estate.

"The Snowfish" by Edward Field. Copyright © 1963 by Edward Field. Reprinted by permission of Edward Field.

"The Rebellion of the Magical Rabbits" by Ariel Dorfman from *Where Angels Glide at Dawn: New Stories from Latin America* edited by Lori M. Carlson and Cynthia L. Ventura. Copyright © 1990 by Ariel Dorfman. Reprinted by permission of HarperCollins Children's Books, a division of HarperCollins Publishers, Inc.

The Story of the Amistad by Emma Gelders Sterne. Copyright © 2001 by Dover Publications, Inc. All rights reserved. Reprinted by permission of Dover Publications, Inc.

Leading Ladies by Marlee Matlin and Doug Cooney. Copyright © 2007 by Marlee Matlin and Doug Cooney. Reprinted by permission of Simon & Schuster Books for Young Readers, an imprint of Simon & Schuster Children's Publishing Division.

"That Something Special: Dancing with the Repertory Dance Company of Harlem" from *Hispanic, Female and Young: An Anthology* edited by Phyllis Tashlik. Copyright © 1994 by Arte Público Press. Reprinted by permission of Arte Público Press–University of Houston.

"Abuela" from *Hispanic, Female and Young: An Anthology* edited by Phyllis Tashlik. Copyright © 1994 by Arte Público Press. Reprinted by permission of Arte Público Press–University of Houston.

"In Music Meeting" by Victoria Forrester. Copyright © 1983 by Victoria Forrester. All rights reserved. Reprinted by permission of the author.

Photo Credits

xiii (bridge) © Fritz Poelking/Elvele Images Ltd/Alamy. **xiii** (frog) © Photospin. **xiii** (shell) © Siede Preis/PhotoDisc. **xiii** (starfish) © Shutterstock. **xiii** (trumpet) © Tony Gable and C Squared Studios/PhotoDisc. **xiii** (guitar) © PhotoDisc. **xiii** (seedlings) © Siede Preis/PhotoDisc. **xiii** (seedling) © Siede Preis/PhotoDisc. **xiii** (rock) © Siede Preis/PhotoDisc. **xiii** (rock) © Siede Preis/PhotoDisc. **xiii** (rocks) © Siede Preis/PhotoDisc. **xiii** (caterpillar) ©